Süss

Süss

Sweet German Treats for Every Occasion

Audrey Leonard
Founder of the Red Currant Bakery blog

PAGE STREET
PUBLISHING CO.

PAGE STREET
PUBLISHING CO.

First published in 2023 by
Page Street Publishing Co.
27 Congress Street, Suite 1511
Salem, MA 01970
www.pagestreetpublishing.com

Distributed by Macmillan, sales in Canada by The Canadian Manda Group.

27   26   25   24   23   1   2   3   4   5

ISBN-13: 978-1-64567-889-2
ISBN-10: 1-64567-889-X

Library of Congress Control Number: 2022950078

Cover and book design by Rosie Stewart for Page Street Publishing Co.
Photography by Audrey Leonard

Printed and bound in China

To my Red Currant Bakery community

CONTENTS

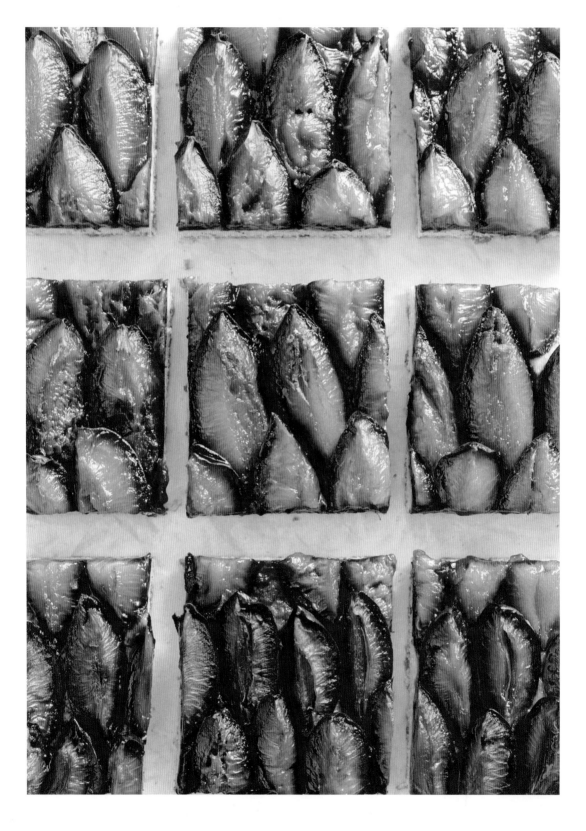

INTRODUCTION

Some of my fondest memories as a kid were the three weeks my mama, sister and I would spend in Munich with my Oma and Opa. Every morning, my sister and I got to go down to the local *bäkerei* (bakery) and pick out what we wanted for breakfast. To me, that was magical—anything I wanted. On special afternoons, we would have *kaffee und kuchen* (coffee and cake), and we would go with either my Oma or Opa to a cafe and get to pick out any slice of cake. To me, that was my candy store. On other days, we would be walking around Munich and stop to get ice cream. As a kid, the food, and especially the sweets, were one of the best parts of every day. As I got older, things like spending time with my grandparents became the priority, but the food was always there. It was always a reason for us to sit down, pause and enjoy each other's company.

COVID hit right as I was graduating from college in New York City. I had just earned a BFA and was planning to work in fashion, but suddenly everything changed. The city and the world shut down. I moved back home with my parents in Colorado and decided to try something new—baking. It wasn't that I decided to be a baker, but rather that I needed something else to focus on, something new to learn. Baking had never been my thing, but my Mama and Oma are both amazing bakers, so I thought maybe I could do it too. I liked cooking because I thought I could be more creative, but baking felt too precise and fussy to me. Turns out that I just had to understand the rules to be able to break them. That's the best part about recipe development— learning everything there is to know about a recipe and then having an idea pop into your head, not for how to make the recipe better, but how to make it "you."

I started baking and almost immediately was drawn to re-creating cakes and pastries I had tasted in Germany. I felt passionate about these recipes because the final product meant something to me. It brought me back to the carefree summer days, eating pastries, cake and ice cream until I was so full I thought someone would have to roll me down the sidewalk, and I knew I wanted to share them. So, I kept going and started posting my images on Instagram to keep track of what I was creating. My page, @redcurrantbakery, was born from my love of red currants, which we used to eat ourselves sick on in Germany every summer, and my love for all things sweet. After a couple of months, I created my blog, Red Currant Bakery, to share complete recipes that I was developing, with as much detail as possible, so that everyone can feel the joy that I feel every time I create a new recipe. It felt amazing to finally be able to share how delicious and beautiful German sweets are with a wider audience.

Every recipe that I create starts with research. Reading about how it was traditionally made, reading how people are making it today, reading recipes from omas (because that's what most of us grow up on). After I understand the recipe, and what makes it so special, I start to test. Then I test and test and test until it's delicious. And then, I test some more, and if I want to change up the flavors, I test even more, until I believe it's as good as it gets without taking it away from its roots.

I wrote this book to share recipes that highlight how magical German baking is, to encourage you to slow down, take the time to bake, but most importantly to take the time to enjoy it with others. If you asked me 2 years ago if I thought I'd write a book, I would've said no before you even finished the question, but now I LOVE to share my recipes with you and hear how much fun you had making them or how you made them for someone from Germany and it brought back so many memories. I wrote this book because I believe that sweets can make anyone's day better and bring people together.

The key to this book is not taking it, or yourself, too seriously. I believe that baking is meant to be fun. You're supposed to make a mess, and you are 100 percent, without a doubt, meant to lick the spatula.

CAKES | Kuchen

Sitting down for an afternoon *kaffee und kuchen* (coffee and cake) is one of my most cherished times of the day. It used to just be memories of summers spent in Germany, but about a year ago, I made a point to start making this afternoon snack daily, and I love it! It forces you to take a break in the day, clear your head and refocus on what the rest of the day will be. Plus, you get to have coffee and cake, so why not?

I'm in a long-term, committed relationship with German cakes. They're not too sweet, just the right amount of creamy, and are often topped with thick layers of buttery streusel. My forever and always, go-to cake is German *Himbeerkuchen* (page 45): a layer of soft and spongy vanilla cake, topped with a vanilla Bavarian cream and finished off with a layer of fresh raspberries and raspberry gel. It's my "I can't decide which cake so I'll go with the classic" cake—I'm never disappointed.

This chapter is your guide to German cakes. It has everything from special occasion cakes to those cakes you make late one night after work, the weekday snack cakes and the cakes you make for weekend breakfast—because we support eating cake for breakfast around here.

MOCHA MOUSSE CAKE | Mokkatorte

This one is for all the chocolate and coffee lovers (myself included). I don't know if I've ever been more excited about a cake recipe! Not only is this cake purely delicious, but it also has two of my favorite things that I need every day: coffee and dark chocolate. The key is making sure both of the flavors are balanced and really come through.

Two layers of rich chocolate sponge cake, layered with a dark chocolate and coffee mousse, then topped with chocolate-covered espresso beans (you can add some to the inside layer of mousse too if you're feeling a little wild). This cake is quite literally not for the faint of heart, but it is delicious, creamy and will, without a doubt, give you a little wake up!

Active Time: 1 hour 30 minutes

Total Time: 24–36 hours

Chocolate Cake

100 g (¾ cup + 1 tbsp) all-purpose flour

50 g (¼ cup + 2 tbsp) cornstarch

65 g (¾ cup) cocoa powder, natural or Dutch processed, plus more for dusting

1 tsp baking powder

3 large eggs, room temperature

200 g (1 cup) granulated sugar

1 tsp vanilla extract

¼ tsp salt

150 ml (½ cup + 2 tbsp) coffee, room temperature

100 ml (6 tbsp + 2 tsp) neutral oil (such as vegetable oil)

100 ml (6 tbsp + 2 tsp) milk

Chocolate Cake

Preheat the oven to 350°F (177°C) and place a rack in the center of the oven. Pour the flour, cornstarch, cocoa powder and baking powder through a fine mesh sieve into a medium-sized mixing bowl. In the bowl of a stand mixer, combine the eggs, sugar, vanilla and salt. Use the whisk attachment to whip on high speed for 3 minutes, until the batter is light and frothy.

In a 2-cup (480-ml) measuring cup, combine the coffee, oil and milk. With the mixer running on medium-low speed, slowly stream the liquids into the beaten eggs. Turn the mixer off and dump in the sifted dry ingredients. Mix again on medium-low speed until everything is just combined. Spray a 9-inch (23-cm) metal springform pan (a 9-inch [23-cm] metal cake pan will work as well) with a baking spray that includes flour or line it with a circle of parchment paper. Pour the batter into the pan and tap it two times on the counter to get rid of the major air bubbles.

Place the cake in the preheated oven and set the timer for 30 minutes. After 30 minutes, rotate the cake and set the timer for 10 more minutes. Check to see if the cake is baked through by quickly inserting a toothpick into the center of the cake and removing it to see if there is wet batter attached to the toothpick. Once it is finished baking, remove the cake from the oven and let it cool for 10 minutes on a wire rack.

After 10 minutes, run a knife along the edge of the cake to loosen it from the sides of the pan.

Release the springform or flip the cake out onto a parchment-lined cooling rack and then flip the cake back, right side up onto another parchment-lined cooling rack. Leave the cake to cool for at least 30 minutes before wrapping it up and putting it in the refrigerator to chill.

(continued)

Mocha Mousse

325 ml (1 cup + 5 tbsp + 2 tsp)
coffee, cold, divided

12 g (1 tbsp + 1 tsp) powdered
gelatin (1.5 packets)

170 g (6 oz) 60% dark chocolate,
finely chopped

100 ml (6 tbsp + 2 tsp) milk

500 ml (2 cups + 1 tbsp + 1 tsp)
heavy whipping cream, cold

6 g (1 heaping tbsp) freshly
ground coffee beans

Chopped chocolate-covered
espresso beans, for decoration,
optional

Mocha Mouse

In a small bowl, add in 75 milliliters (5 tbsp) of cold coffee and sprinkle in the 12 grams (1 tbsp + 1 tsp) of gelatin. Stir to combine and set aside.

In a large, heat-safe bowl, add in the finely chopped chocolate. In a medium sauce pot, add in the remaining coffee and milk. Heat over medium heat, stirring occasionally for 5 to 10 minutes, until it just begins to bubble. Take the pot off the heat and pour the liquid into the bowl with the chopped chocolate. Use a whisk to stir until the chocolate has fully melted into the liquid. Quickly add the bloomed gelatin into the coffee-chocolate mixture and whisk again until it has all dissolved.

Set the bowl aside to cool to room temperature (this should take 1 to 2 hours). You will want to stir it and scrape the sides of the bowl often to keep it from clumping. If you want to move the process along, create an ice bath by placing the bowl into a larger baking dish with tall sides and adding ice and water into the baking dish around the bowl. This means you will need to stir the mixture frequently but it will also cool down much faster. The mixture needs to be fully cooled but not stiff before you fold in the whipped cream.

Once cooled to room temperature, add the cold heavy whipping cream with the ground coffee into the bowl of a stand mixer. Use the whisk attachment to whip the cream on medium-high speed until stiff peaks form. In two additions, add the chocolate-coffee liquid into the whipped cream. Use a wide, flat rubber spatula to fold the chocolate into the whipped cream. Don't stir the mixture or you will deflate the cream and make a dense filling.

Once the cake has chilled, take it out of the refrigerator and use a long, serrated knife to cut it into two equal layers and level off the top if it is not flat. The top of the cake can be a little sticky on your hand, so I recommend laying a sheet of parchment or plastic wrap on the top of the cake while cutting it. For the cleanest lines, use an adjustable cake collar or acetate collar to assemble.

On a plate or small tray, lay down a sheet of plastic wrap. Place the bottom layer of cake onto the lined plate with the cut side face up and then wrap the collar around the chocolate cake so that it is snug around the cake but not squishing it, as it will then be difficult to fit the top layer in. Use a ladle to scoop approximately half of the *mokka* cream over the chocolate cake. Use the back of the ladle to smooth out the layer and bring it all the way to the edges.

Place the top layer of cake over it with the cut side face down. Press down on the top layer of cake so that it lies level and firmly on the mousse. Pour the remaining mousse over the second layer of cake and carefully place the cake back in the refrigerator for at least 8 hours or overnight.

Once it is set, take the cake out of the refrigerator and peel away the collar.

Optionally, chop up a handful of dark chocolate-covered espresso beans and sprinkle them on top of the cake.

Slice the cake with a long thin knife. It is best if you run the knife under hot water between each slice because it will both clean the knife and heat it up, making it easier to cut through the chilled cake.

Notes

Don't rush the chilling times on this cake. If anything is too warm when assembled, it will melt and you won't get that light and fluffy mousse texture.

This cake can be made a day or two in advance, but I recommend eating it within 4 or 5 days.

AUSTRIAN CHOCOLATE APRICOT TORTE | Sachertorte

Servings: 8–12

While *Sachertorte* is traditionally from Austria, it has become so popular that you can find it almost anywhere in Germany. One of my favorite cafes in Munich has a version of the classic that includes a little marzipan (stick with me) and rum, along with the traditional apricot jam, in the filling to keep the cake rich and moist without deviating too much from the classic Austrian flavor.

While I enjoy the classic, which sticks to just apricot jam between the layers, it can sometimes be a little dry, and I immediately fell in love with the addition of rum and marzipan. Don't be turned off by the marzipan—even my mom who hates marzipan likes this cake! Traditionally, the coating is a chocolate simple syrup, but I love the taste of dark chocolate ganache and have used that to coat this torte instead for a richer and more chocolatey flavor.

Active Time: 1 hour

Total Time: 3 hours

Chocolate Cake

6 large eggs, cold

150 g (⅔ cup) butter

150 g (5.3 oz) 60% dark chocolate

150 g (¾ cup) granulated sugar

1 tsp vanilla extract

125 g (1 cup) all-purpose flour

21 g (2 tbsp + 2 tsp) cornstarch

1 tsp baking powder

¼ tsp salt

Chocolate Cake

Preheat the oven to 350°F (177°C) and place a rack in the center of the oven. Separate the whites from the yolks of all 6 eggs. Place the whites in the bowl of a stand mixer and the yolks in a separate large mixing bowl. Set both aside.

In a microwave-safe bowl, melt the butter and chocolate together in 20-second intervals, stirring in between. Whisk the egg yolks, sugar and vanilla extract together in a separate bowl. Place the bowl on a damp towel and slowly pour in the melted chocolate and butter mixture while whisking constantly. Add the flour, cornstarch and baking powder into the chocolate mixture and mix again until just combined.

Pour the salt into the egg whites in the bowl of the stand mixer. Use a whisk attachment on medium speed until the egg whites become frothy. Turn the speed to high and whip until stiff peaks form, for 5 minutes. Fold the egg whites into the chocolate mixture in three additions. Be sure to use a gentle folding motion with a rubber spatula rather than stirring them to prevent the egg whites from deflating. Fold until no more white flecks remain.

Line a 9-inch (23-cm) springform pan (a 9-inch [23-cm] metal cake pan will work too) with a baking spray that includes flour. Just be sure to not overspray it or let much come up the sides of the pan. Alternatively, you can lightly grease the base with butter and then lay a circle of parchment paper on top. Pour the cake batter into the pan. If you see white flecks of egg white when pouring the batter in, don't worry—it will be ok when you bake it. Place the cake in the preheated oven and set the timer for 30 minutes.

After 30 minutes have passed, rotate the pan 180 degrees and bake for another 20 minutes, until a toothpick inserted in the center of the cake comes out clean. Once baked, remove the cake from the oven and place it on a wire rack to cool for at least 10 to 15 minutes. Run a knife along the edge between the cake and the pan to make sure that it didn't stick anywhere and then release the springform. Leave the cake to cool fully to room temperature (this will take 2 to 3 hours). It will absorb the soak and filling if you do it at room temperature and don't first put the cake in the refrigerator.

(continued)

Simple Syrup Soak

100 ml (6 tbsp + 2 tsp) water

100 g (½ cup) granulated sugar

Filling

250 g (¾ cup + ½ tbsp) apricot jam

45 ml (3 tbsp) rum

140 g (½ cup + 2 tbsp) marzipan

Topping

170 g (6 oz) 60% dark chocolate

177 ml (6 oz) heavy whipping cream

Simple Syrup Soak

In a small sauce pot, combine the water and sugar. Turn the heat to medium-low and stir regularly until the sugar has fully dissolved into the water. Once dissolved, remove the syrup from the heat and set aside.

Filling

In a separate pot, add in the jam, rum and marzipan broken into small pieces. Turn the heat to low and stir, gently mashing the marzipan into the mixture, until it is completely smooth. Set aside to cool slightly, for 5 to 10 minutes, stirring frequently.

Using a long, serrated knife, trim off the top of the cooled cake to level it out and then cut it in half. Use a ladle or pastry brush to evenly distribute the simple syrup over the top surface of each layer of cake.

Place the bottom layer of the cake onto a lined plate or tray with parchment paper or plastic wrap. If available, wrap the cake with a removable cake collar or acetate collar. Pour half of the apricot filling over the bottom layer of cake and spread evenly. Place the second layer of the cake on top of the apricot filling and pour the remaining filling over the second layer. Smooth the filling out as best you can and place the cake in the refrigerator for at least 30 minutes to cool.

Topping

While the cake cools, make the chocolate coating. Chop up the chocolate into ¼-inch (6-mm) bits and place in a large heat-safe bowl. Heat the heavy whipping cream in a small pot until just simmering, for 5 to 10 minutes, stirring frequently to prevent it from burning. Once hot, pour the cream over the chocolate and leave it to sit for 1 minute. Use a whisk to combine the cream and chocolate until smooth.

Take the cake out of the refrigerator and remove the collar. Place the cake on an upside down bowl, whose base is slightly smaller than that of the cake. Pour the chocolate coating over the top of the cake working in a spiral motion from the center out.

Use an offset spatula to smooth out the chocolate and bring it over the sides so that it coats the sides of the cake. Be careful not to press too hard or you will catch some of the apricot filling.

Allow the excess chocolate to run off the sides of the cake and then use the offset spatula to cleanly wipe off any remaining drips.

Transfer the cake to a cake plate or stand for serving. Place the cake in the refrigerator for 30 minutes to allow the chocolate to set. Use a long sharp knife to cut the slices. Run the knife under hot water between each slice to clean it off and to make it easier to cut through the chocolate coating.

Notes

Unlike most cakes, this cake should be cut and assembled while still at room temperature. If the cake is chilled first, it doesn't absorb the soak and jam as well, which means that the layers of cake don't hold together as well, either.

If you want to go the chocolate simple syrup route, there are many recipes online, and they would work on top of this cake instead of the ganache.

DOUBLE CHOCOLATE CHERRY STREUSEL CAKE | Schokolade Kirschkuchen

Servings: 8–12

This is one of those casual late night or weekend morning kinds of cakes; it's perfect for snacking on during the week or as a chocolatey addition to breakfast. It's simple, with everything baked together in one pan, no post-baking assembly required; it's the kind of cake that just makes your heart happy and puts your soul at peace. Plus, you can never go wrong with a chocolate-cherry combo inspired by the classic German *Schwarzwälder Kirschtorte*.

Rich chocolate cake with tart cherries folded in, topped with more cherries and a chocolate streusel, creates not only a yummy balance of flavors but also textures. It's best served a little warm with a dusting of powdered sugar and a drizzle of Vanille Soße (page 140).

Baking Time: 1 hour

Total Time: 1 hour 30 minutes

Chocolate Streusel

85 g (⅔ cup) all-purpose flour

100 g (½ cup) granulated sugar

18 g (3 tbsp + 1 tsp) cocoa powder

1 tsp kosher salt

100 g (⅓ cup + 1 tbsp) butter, softened

1 tsp vanilla extract

Chocolate Cake

70 g (2.5 oz) 60% dark chocolate

150 g (1 cup + 3 tbsp) all-purpose flour

150 g (¾ cup) granulated sugar

12 g (2 tbsp + 1 tsp) cocoa powder, Dutch processed

½ tsp baking soda

½ tsp baking powder

½ tsp kosher salt

2 large eggs, room temperature

125 g (½ cup + 2 tsp) butter, softened

125 ml (½ cup + 1 tsp) yogurt, room temperature

1 tsp vanilla extract

285 g (1½ cups + 2 tbsp) canned tart cherries, drained, divided

Chocolate Streusel

In a medium-sized bowl, whisk together the flour, sugar, cocoa powder and salt. Add in the softened butter and vanilla extract. Use a fork or your hands to rub the butter into the dry ingredients. Continue to mix until no dry bits remain and the mixture clumps easily.

Chocolate Cake

Preheat the oven to 350°F (177°C) and place a rack in the center of the oven. Melt the dark chocolate in a small microwave-safe bowl in short bursts and set aside to cool slightly. Add the flour, sugar, cocoa powder, baking soda, baking powder and salt into the bowl of a stand mixer. Whisk to combine. Add in the eggs, butter, yogurt and vanilla. Use the paddle attachment, first on low and then on high, to mix the batter until it is smooth and fluffy, for 2 minutes. Pour the melted chocolate in and scrape down the sides and bottom of the bowl with a rubber spatula. Mix again until the batter is just combined.

Take the bowl off the mixer and pour in 160 grams (¾ cup + 2½ tbsp) of the drained cherries. Use a rubber spatula to fold them into the batter. Spray a 9-inch (23-cm) metal springform pan (a 9-inch [23-cm] metal cake pan will work as well) with a baking spray that includes flour or line with a circle of parchment paper. Pour the batter into the pan. Crumble the chocolate streusel over the top of the cake. Sprinkle the remaining cherries over top of the streusel.

Place the cake in the preheated oven and set the timer for 40 minutes. After 40 minutes, rotate the cake and set the timer for 20 more minutes. Check to see if the cake is baked through by quickly inserting a toothpick into the center of the cake and removing it to see if there is wet batter attached to the toothpick. After it is finished baking, remove the cake from the oven and let it cool for 10 minutes on a wire rack. After 10 minutes, run a knife along the edge of the cake to loosen it from the sides of the pan.

Release the springform and let the cake cool for at least 20 more minutes before serving. If using a metal cake pan, I recommend letting the cake cool for longer in the pan before trying to lift it out with a spatula or serving it straight from the pan. Optionally, dust the cake with a little powdered sugar before serving.

FRUIT & CREAM TORTE | Obsttorte

An *Obsttorte* is really any type of fruit tart, but in Germany, most people will think of either a vanilla sponge or vanilla shortcrust base filled with a vanilla cream or pudding and topped with fresh fruit. This is one of those low-effort, high-impact kinds of cakes because it's always stunning to look at but so easy to make and so versatile depending on which fruits are in season.

This Obsttorte has a light vanilla sponge base, a vanilla and lemon mousse-like filling and a fresh berry topping. It's quick, it's easy, but still a show-stopper. If you are in stone fruit season, this would be DELISH with fresh peaches and plums or even apricots. Or, you could swap out the vanilla pudding for a chocolate pudding, leave out the lemon juice, and add fresh pitted cherries to the top for a more decadent version!

Active Time: 20 minutes

Total Time: 2 hours

Vanilla Cake

3 large eggs, room temperature

85 g (6 tbsp) granulated sugar

80 g (5 tbsp + 2 tsp) butter, melted and slightly cooled

100 g (¾ cup + 1 tbsp) all-purpose flour

1 tsp baking powder

Vanilla Cake

Preheat the oven to 350°F (177°C) and place a rack in the center of the oven. In the bowl of a stand mixer, add in the eggs and sugar and whisk on high with the whisk attachment until the mixture is light and fluffy, between 3 and 5 minutes. Turn the mixer down to medium-low speed and stream in the melted butter down the inside of the bowl. Continue to whisk until just combined.

Remove the bowl from the mixer and use a sieve to sift in the flour and baking powder. Hold the whisk attachment from the mixer in your hand and use it in a scooping and folding motion to mix the dry ingredients into the wet. Continue to mix until all ingredients are combined and use a rubber spatula for the sides and bottom of the bowl if necessary. Spray a classic *Obstboden* pan with non-stick baking spray that has flour in it.

Pour the cake batter into the pan and place the cake in the preheated oven. Set the timer for 10 minutes. Once baked, remove the cake from the oven and place on a wire rack to cool for at least 10 to 15 minutes. Place a sheet of parchment paper over the top and then a plate or a second wire rack upside down on top of the parchment paper. In one swift movement, holding on to the cake pan, the parchment paper and the plate or rack, flip the cake over so the cake releases from the pan onto the parchment paper. If it doesn't release, flip the pan back over and use a butter knife or your fingers to gently loosen the edges of the cake away from the pan.

Leave the cake to cool fully to room temperature. If you are not assembling the cake that day, wrap it in plastic wrap and refrigerate until cold.

(continued)

Vanilla Cream Layer

Vanilla Cream Layer

175 ml (¾ cup) milk, cold

70 g (6 tbsp + 1 tsp) instant vanilla pudding mix

15 ml (1 tbsp) lemon juice

125 ml (½ cup + 1 tsp) heavy whipping cream, cold

In a medium-sized bowl, pour in the cold milk and sprinkle over the vanilla pudding mix. Use a whisk to whisk the pudding mixture together constantly for 3 minutes. This can also be done with a machine. The pudding will become quite thick. Then whisk in 15 milliliters (1 tbsp) of lemon juice.

In a separate bowl, pour in the cold heavy cream. Use an electric mixer to whip the cream on medium-high speed until medium stiff peaks form. In two additions, use a wide and flat rubber spatula to fold the whipped cream into the vanilla pudding. The first addition will allow the pudding to soften and be more fluid and the second will make it nice and fluffy. Once combined, spoon or pour the cream into the center indentation of the cake. Use the back of a spoon or a spatula to smooth it into a flat layer. Place in the refrigerator for 30 minutes before adding the fruit on top.

Fresh Fruit Layer

400–500 g (14.1–17.6 oz) fresh berries

Fresh Fruit Layer

Rinse and pat dry the fresh berries or your fruit of choice. If using strawberries, remove the stems and the center core. Arrange the fruit onto the vanilla cream layer in your desired design. If served immediately, the cream will be a little soft and likely squish out as you cut it but will still be delicious. If you want it to be a little more set, leave it in the refrigerator for a couple hours or up to overnight. Optionally, dust the top with powdered sugar just before serving.

Notes

This cake is traditionally made with an Obstboden pan that creates an indentation in the top of the cake. However, I have also tested it in a 10-inch (25-cm) springform pan, and it works as well—just don't spread the filling all the way to the edge of the cake and let it set for an hour or two in the refrigerator before adding the fresh berries on top.

This version is topped with only raspberries, blueberries, and blackberries but the opportunities are endless. You can top it with anything from pitted cherries, to red currants, to star fruit or even sauteed and cooled apples.

This recipe will also work with a pudding mix that needs to be cooked.

CHOCOLATE & VANILLA CREAM CAKE SLICES | Milchschnitte

Servings: 12–16

Directly translated, *Milchschnitte* means "milk slices," which makes sense because the filling has a milky cream taste to it, but they're so much more than that. Milchschnitte are one of those treats that kids get in Germany, individually wrapped at the local grocery store or newsstand on their way home from school. Whether you've had Milchschnitte before or not, you can't help but feel like a kid when you eat these light and airy slices with your hands like an ice cream sandwich. Made with two layers of thin chocolate cake sandwiched with a stiff vanilla cream, they're the perfect little sweet snack or a fun dessert to finish off a warm summer night.

Active Time: 45 minutes

Total Time: 8 hours

Chocolate Cake

56 g (¼ cup + 3 tbsp)
all-purpose flour

12 g (1½ tbsp) cornstarch

½ tsp baking powder

25 g (3 tbsp + 2 tsp) cocoa
powder, Dutch processed

4 large eggs, room temperature

64 g (4½ tbsp) granulated sugar

Chocolate Cake

Preheat the oven to 350°F (177°C) and place a rack in the middle of the oven. Line an 18 x 13–inch (46 x 33–cm) baking sheet with parchment paper (all the way to the edges) or a silicone baking mat. Sift the flour, cornstarch, baking powder and cocoa powder into a medium bowl and set aside.

Crack all four eggs into the bowl of a stand mixer. Use the whisk attachment to whisk on high for 3 to 5 minutes, until the eggs are very fluffy and tripled in volume. Turn the mixer down to medium and sprinkle in the granulated sugar. Turn the mixer back up to high and mix again for 2 minutes. Take the bowl off the mixer and dump in the sifted dry ingredients. Use a wide, flat spatula to gently fold the dry ingredients into the whipped eggs.

Pour the fully mixed chocolate batter onto the lined baking sheet, evenly down the center lengthwise. With the rubber spatula or an offset spatula, carefully spread the batter to the edges of the pan. Bake the cake in the preheated oven for 12 minutes.

After 12 minutes, take the pan out of the oven and place it on a wire rack. Immediately, run a knife along the edge of the cake to loosen it from the pan. Place a second sheet of parchment over the cake and then flip a second baking sheet upside down over everything so that the edges of both pans are lined up and the cake isn't squished. Holding onto both pans (you'll want potholders for this), flip the pans over so that the cake tips into the cold pan. Take the top, hot pan off and gently peel away the silicone baking mat or parchment paper. Leave the cake to cool fully while preparing the filling—this will only take 10 to 15 minutes because the cake is so thin.

(continued)

Cream Filling

75 ml (5 tbsp) milk, cold

7–8 g (2 tsp) powdered gelatin
(1 packet)

400 ml (1½ cups + 2 tbsp +
2 tsp) heavy whipping cream,
divided

75 g (5 tbsp) powdered sugar

Cream Filling

In a medium-sized heat-safe bowl, stir together the cold milk and gelatin. Set aside.

In a small sauce pot, add in 150 milliliters (½ cup + 2 tablespoons) of the cream and heat it over medium heat for 5 to 10 minutes, stirring frequently, until it is steaming. Turn the heat off and pour the hot cream into the bloomed gelatin. Whisk to allow the bloomed gelatin to dissolve into the hot cream. Allow the mixture to cool to room temperature, stirring frequently to allow it to cool evenly without clumping.

Once cooled, pour the remaining cold whipping cream into the bowl of a stand mixer with the powdered sugar. Use an electric mixer with the whisk attachment to whip the cream, first on medium-low until the powdered sugar is mixed in and then increasing the speed to medium-high until stiff peaks form. Pour the cooled gelatin mixture onto the whipped cream and fold to combine.

Cut the cooled cake in half so that you now have two rectangles that are 13 x 9 inch (33 x 23 cm). Scoop the cream filling onto one half of the cake and spread into an even layer within a ¼ inch (6 mm) of the edge of the cake. If the filling is a little soft and too runny to hold its shape, place the bowl in the refrigerator for 5-minute increments until it is stiff enough to spread.

Place the second rectangle of cake over the top of the filling and press it down gently so the filling squeezes all the way to the edges. Place the cake in the refrigerator for at least 4 hours or up to overnight to set. Once set, use a long, sharp knife to trim away the edges. Then, cut the cake in half lengthwise, parallel with the longer sides. Clean the knife between each cut for neat slices.

Then, turn the pan 90 degrees and cut it into sixths or eighths perpendicular to the cuts you have just made. You will be left with 12 or 16 slices depending on the size you chose.

Note

These are best stored in an airtight container in the refrigerator and can be kept there for up to a week, if they last that long.

CHOCOLATE RASPBERRY ROULADE | Himbeer Schokolade Roulade

Makes: 12 slices

Chocolate on chocolate on chocolate with a little raspberry to balance things out, this Chocolate Raspberry Roulade is a chocolate lover's dream. In Germany, roulades can be sweet or savory and are really used to describe anything rolled up with filling. Not surprisingly, my favorites are always the sweet variations, often made with a fatless sponge cake and filled with some sort of cream or fruit.

This recipe was inspired by my love for chocolate and raspberries with a light chocolate sponge rolled with whipped chocolate ganache and fresh raspberries, and then dusted with a little cocoa powder. This cake is the perfect centerpiece for a dinner party or even as your next birthday cake! If you want to go FULL CHOCOLATE, leave out the raspberries for an extra decadent dessert.

Active Time: 1 hour

Total Time: 24 hours

Cake

30 g (¼ cup + 2 tbsp) cocoa powder, natural or Dutch processed, plus more for dusting

75 g (½ cup + 1 tbsp + 1 tsp) all-purpose flour

20 g (2 tbsp + 2 tsp) cornstarch

5 egg whites

6 egg yolks

140 g (⅔ cup + 2 tsp) granulated sugar, divided

1 tsp vanilla extract

38 ml (3 tbsp) vegetable oil

¼ tsp salt

Cake

Preheat the oven to 350°F (177°C) and place a rack in the center of the oven. Line a baking sheet with a silicone baking mat or a sheet of parchment paper. Sift the cocoa powder, flour and cornstarch into a medium bowl.

Place 5 egg whites into the bowl of a stand mixer and 6 egg yolks into a separate medium bowl. Add 70 grams (¼ cup + 1½ tbsp) of the sugar into the bowl with the egg whites. Beat the egg whites with the whisk attachment first on medium-low speed until they are frothy and then increase the speed to medium-high for 5 minutes, until stiff peaks form, but this can take longer.

Just before the egg whites have hit stiff peaks, add the remaining 70 grams (¼ cup + 1½ tbsp) of sugar, vanilla, oil, and salt into the bowl with the egg yolks and whisk until everything is fully combined. Once stiff peaks have formed, remove the bowl from the mixer and pour the whisked egg yolks on top. Fold the egg yolks into the egg whites until they are fully combined, being careful not to knock all of the air out of the whites. Pour the sifted dry ingredients into the egg mixture and fold to combine.

Pour the mixed batter onto the lined baking sheet. Lightly spread the batter over the baking sheet all the way to the edges. Make the cake as even as possible as it won't spread as it bakes. Bake the cake in the preheated oven for 12 minutes. Remove the baking sheet from the oven and place it on a cooling rack for 3 minutes.

Gently run a dinner knife along all edges of the baking sheet to loosen the cake from the edges of the baking sheet. Dust the surface of the cake with cocoa powder or powdered sugar and lay a sheet of parchment paper over the surface of the cake. Holding the parchment to the edges of the baking sheet, flip the baking sheet over so that the cake can fall away, onto a towel.

Starting at one short edge, roll the cake between the towel and parchment paper or baking mat all the way to the other end. Once rolled, set the cake aside to cool fully to room temperature before filling—this can take a few hours.

(continued)

Filling

226 g (½ lb) 60% dark chocolate, finely chopped

360 ml (12 fl oz) heavy cream

150 g (5.3 oz) fresh raspberries, rinsed and patted dry

30 g (6 tbsp) cocoa powder or powdered sugar, for dusting

Filling

Once the cake has cooled, make the filling. In a medium-sized heat-safe bowl, add in the finely chopped dark chocolate. In a medium sauce pot, heat the heavy cream until it is steaming, stirring frequently, for 5 to 10 minutes. Once hot, pour the cream over the chocolate and let it sit for about 1 minute. After the minute has passed, whisk the cream and chocolate together until the mixture is completely smooth. This mixture needs to come to room temperature before whipping it, so continue to whisk it every 10 to 15 minutes, until it is cooled, 30 minutes to 1 hour depending on your room temperature.

Using a handheld mixer or a stand mixer fitted with a whisk attachment, whip the chocolate ganache (starting low and moving to high speed) until lines form. Working quickly, fold the rinsed raspberries into the chocolate ganache. Unroll the cake gently and peel off the parchment paper or baking mat. Spread the whipped chocolate ganache and raspberries onto the cooled cake, leaving a ¾-inch (2-cm) border on the short end that won't be the center of the roll.

Use the towel to help roll the cake back up with the filling, follow the same roll direction as it was when it cooled, but don't roll the towel into the cake. Once tightly rolled, place the cake in the refrigerator to set for 1 to 2 hours. Once it is set, trim off both ends of the roll to make neat spirals. Dust the cake with powdered sugar or cocoa powder. Slice the cake into 12 (1-inch [2.5-cm]) slices.

Note

Once the chocolate ganache has been whipped, it needs to be spread on the cake immediately; if it sits out for too long, it will cool and become too stiff to spread.

RED CURRANT MERINGUE TORTE |
Johannisbeer–Baiser Torte

Servings: 12

If you're looking for something light and fruity, I have a feeling you'll like this German torte. I had a slice of *Johannisbeer-Baiser* torte for the first time on my most recent trip to Germany (because as we've already established, I used to exclusively eat *Himbeerkuchen* as a kid) and immediately questioned why I hadn't been eating it for years. It's such a perfect summer cake and very classically German with the meringue topping and red currant filling. Made with a vanilla sponge cake base, layered with a cooked-down red currant compote filling, and topped with a mountain of torched meringue, the combination of the tart red currants with the soft and sweet meringue is a match made in heaven.

Active Time: 1 hour 30 minutes

Total Time: 24 hours

Vanilla Cake

3 large eggs, room temperature

135 g (½ cup + 3 tbsp) granulated sugar

¼ tsp salt

1 tsp vanilla extract

1 lemon, zested

100 ml (⅓ cup + 2 tbsp) butter, melted and cooled slightly

100 g (¾ cup + 1 tbsp) all-purpose flour

1 tsp baking powder

Vanilla Cake

Preheat the oven to 350°F (177°C) and place a rack in the center of the oven. In the bowl of a stand mixer, add in the eggs, sugar, salt, vanilla and lemon zest. Whisk on high with the whisk attachment until light and fluffy and lines begin to form as the whisk passes through, about 3 to 5 minutes. Turn the mixer down to medium-low speed and stream in the melted and cooled butter down the inside of the bowl. Continue to whisk until everything is just combined.

Remove the bowl from the mixer and sift in the flour and baking powder with a fine mesh sieve. Hold the whisk attachment from the mixer in your hand and use it in a scooping and folding motion to mix the dry ingredients into the wet. Continue to mix until all ingredients are combined and use a rubber spatula for the sides and bottom of the bowl if necessary.

Line a 9 x 9–inch (23 x 23–cm) square metal pan with a baking spray that includes flour—just be sure to not overspray it or let much come up the sides of the pan. Alternatively, you can lightly grease the base and two opposite sides with butter and then lay a rectangle of parchment that is 9 x 16–inch (23 x 41–cm) over the greased portions of the pan. Pour the cake batter into the pan and place the cake in the preheated oven. Set the timer for 20 minutes.

After 20 minutes have passed, check to see if it is golden brown and a toothpick inserted in the center comes out clean. Another way to tell if it is done baking is to look and see if the edges of the cake are pulling away from the pan. If not, bake for 5 more minutes.

Once baked, remove the cake from the oven and place it on a wire rack to cool for at least 10 to 15 minutes. Then, run a knife along the edge between the cake and the pan to make sure that it didn't stick anywhere. If lined with parchment paper, use both sides to gently lift the cake out and place it on a wire cooling rack. If not, place a sheet of parchment paper over the top and gently tip the cake out and then place it top side up on a wire rack with a piece of parchment paper between the cake and the rack. Leave the cake to cool fully to room temperature. Wrap in plastic wrap and refrigerate until cold.

(continued)

Red Currant Layer

36 g (¼ cup + ½ tbsp) cornstarch

150 g (¾ cup) granulated sugar

100 ml (¼ cup + 1 tbsp + 1 tsp) water

10 ml (2 tsp) lemon juice

900 g (6 cups + 3 tbsp) frozen red currants, divided

Meringue

4 egg whites (120 g)

¼ teaspoon salt

200 g (1 cup) sugar

Notes

This cake is made with frozen red currants because I have found that they are easier to come by in the US at European grocery stores. If you can find them fresh that's great, too, and if you have too many, freeze the extra for when they're no longer in season!

This cake is somewhat delicate once cut so I recommend cutting it on the dish you plan to serve from or inside of the pan and then using a small spatula to lift the slices out.

Red Currant Layer

In a medium-sized heavy-bottomed sauce pot, add in the cornstarch and sugar and whisk to combine. Slowly pour in the water and lemon juice while whisking until a smooth paste forms. Pour in 600 grams (2 cups + 1 tbsp) of the red currants and turn the heat to medium. Use a rubber spatula to stir the mixture frequently as it cooks. Continue to cook until the mixture has thickened and begins to bubble, for 10 to 15 minutes. Then, cook for at least 5 more minutes, stirring constantly. Remove the pot from the heat and stir in the remaining red currants. Pour the mixture into a large shallow bowl to allow it to come to room temperature–this can take an hour or two.

While the red currant mixture cools, prepare the cake. Clean the 9 x 9–inch (23 x 23–cm) pan from before and line it with another parchment paper sling–there is no need to grease the pan first this time. Using a long serrated knife, cut the vanilla cake into two even layers. If this seems daunting, you can always cut the cake in half and then cut each half into two layers because we will be slicing the cake into squares after assembly anyway. Place the bottom layer of cake with the cut side face up into the lined pan. Spread the cooled red currant filling over the top and then lay the top layer of cake, cut side down, over the filling. Press down gently so the cake is level and place in the refrigerator overnight to set.

Meringue

In the bowl of a stand mixer, combine the egg whites, salt and sugar. Heat 2 inches (5 cm) of water in a medium-sized saucepan. Once just barely simmering, place the bowl with egg whites and sugar over the pot; it should be big enough to just sit on top of the pot. Use a whisk to whisk the egg whites and sugar together. Keep whisking for 5 to 10 minutes, until the sugar dissolves into the egg whites. You can test this by rubbing some between your fingers to see if you still feel grains of sugar. The mixture should also be quite warm. Once it reaches this point, place the bowl on the mixer and use the whisk attachment to whisk on medium until the mixture is frothy. Then, increase the speed to high and whisk until stiff, shiny peaks form and the bottom of the bowl feels like it has returned to room temperature.

Take the cake out of the refrigerator and lift it out of the pan onto the plate or dish you want to serve it from. Scoop the meringue over the cake and swirl in your desired pattern with a spoon or spatula. Optionally, torch the tops of the peaks of meringue with a blow torch.

Slice the cake into 16 squares by cutting it in half both lengthwise and widthwise with a long, thin, sharp knife and then cutting each half in half again. Be sure to clean the knife between each slice.

CHOCOLATE WALNUT BUNDT CAKE | Schoko Walnuss Gugelhupf

Servings: 12–16

A *Gugelhupf* is really another name for a Bundt cake. Traditionally, Gugelhupfs are raised with yeast rather than baking soda or baking powder, but nowadays people use the names interchangeably. A traditional German Gugelhupf is made with a plain vanilla yeasted cake, studded with dried fruit and dusted with powdered sugar. Contrary to what you might think, the addition of yeast doesn't make the cake tough and bread-like—it just gives it a slightly different flavor.

This recipe has dark chocolate added in three different ways and toasted walnuts mixed into the batter for crunch and flavor. This one, without a doubt, falls into the category of an anytime cake. You could have it for breakfast with coffee, with an afternoon coffee or even for dessert after dinner!

Active Time: 45 minutes

Total Time: 3 hours

Cake

113 g (4 oz) 60% chocolate

100 g (¾ cup + 1 tbsp) walnuts, plus more for topping

425 g (3 cups + ⅓ cup + 1 tbsp) all-purpose flour

150 g (¾ cup) granulated sugar

12 g (1 tbsp) instant yeast (1½ packets)

175 ml (⅔ cup + 1 tbsp) whole milk, lukewarm

2 large eggs, room temperature

200 g (¾ cup + 2 tbsp) butter, softened

1 tsp vanilla extract

165 g (5.8 oz) 60% dark chocolate chips or chunks

Chocolate Topping

250 g (8.8 oz) 60% dark chocolate, melted

Cake

Prepare the chocolate bar by chopping it into fine pieces, almost shaving-sized. Then, toast the walnuts in a pan over medium heat until the oils begin to appear and the nuts become slightly browned. Roughly chop the nuts and set them aside.

In the bowl of a stand mixer, whisk the flour, sugar and yeast together. Pour in the lukewarm milk, eggs, softened butter and vanilla. Using the dough hook attachment, knead the dough on medium-low speed until just combined, for 5 to 10 minutes. Pour the finely chopped chocolate into the bowl and knead again briefly until it is just mixed in.

Take the bowl from the mixer and pour in the chocolate chips or chunks and the roughly chopped walnuts. Use a rubber spatula or bowl scraper to mix the add-ins in. Spray a Bundt pan with a baking spray that has flour in it. Scoop the dough out of the bowl and into the lined pan. Try to get the dough as evenly distributed as possible. Cover the pan with a sheet of plastic wrap and set it somewhere warm to rise for at least 1 hour.

Preheat the oven to 350°F (177°C) and place a rack in the center of the oven. Once the dough has grown at least an inch or two (2.5 to 5 cm) in the pan, remove the plastic wrap and place it in the preheated oven. Set a timer for 25 minutes. After the 25 minutes have passed, rotate the cake 180 degrees and bake for another 15 to 20 minutes, until it is golden brown.

Once baked, remove the pan from the oven and set it on a wire rack to cool for 30 to 40 minutes. Once the pan is cool to the touch, place a second wire rack over the top of the pan. Holding onto both the pan and the second wire rack, flip the pan over. The cake should fall out of the pan. If not, try tapping a few times on the pan to get it to release. If it still doesn't come out, flip the cake back over and use a butter knife or a skewer to try to loosen the edges of the cake from the pan and try to flip it over again.

Chocolate Topping

Allow the cake to cool fully before topping with melted chocolate and walnuts. This cake is best cut with a serrated knife once the chocolate has set but it can also be cut while the chocolate is still melted.

RASPBERRY ICE CREAM CHOCOLATE CAKE |
Himbeereis Torte

Eistorten a.k.a. ice cream cakes are often made with two layers of actual sponge cake with another layer of ice cream in between, unlike in the US, where they are often made with a brownie or cookie base and then topped with ice cream. I find the German version to be much lighter and more refreshing on a hot summer day!

One of my favorite parts about this cake is how creative you can be with it. You can fill the cake with any type of ice cream—did someone say coffee *stracciatella*? Or you could do a swirled combination of a couple of different flavors! I love to keep it simple and just dust the top with cocoa powder but you could also add a layer of whipped cream or a drizzle of chocolate sauce if you're feeling decadent.

Active Time: 45 minutes
Total Time: 24 hours

Chocolate Cake

100 g (¾ cup + 1 tbsp) all-purpose flour

50 g (¼ cup + 2 tbsp) cornstarch

65 g (¾ cup) cocoa powder natural or Dutch processed, plus more for dusting

1 tsp baking powder

3 large eggs, room temperature

200 g (1 cup) granulated sugar

1 tsp vanilla extract

¼ tsp salt

150 ml (½ cup + 2 tbsp) coffee, room temperature

100 ml (¼ cup + 2 tbsp) neutral oil (such as vegetable oil)

100 ml (¼ cup + 2 tbsp) milk

Chocolate Cake

Preheat the oven to 350°F (177°C) and place a rack in the center of the oven. Pour the flour, cornstarch, cocoa powder and baking powder through a fine mesh sieve into a medium-sized mixing bowl. In the bowl of a stand mixer, combine the eggs, sugar, vanilla and salt. Use the whisk attachment to whip on high speed for 3 minutes, until the mixture is light and frothy.

In a 2-cup (480-ml) measuring cup, combine the coffee, oil and milk. With the mixer running on medium-low speed, slowly stream the liquids into the beaten eggs. Turn the mixer off and dump in the sifted dry ingredients. Mix again on medium-low speed until all the ingredients are just combined.

Spray a 9-inch (23-cm) metal springform pan (a 9-inch [23-cm] metal cake pan will work as well) with a baking spray that includes flour or line with a circle of parchment paper. Pour the batter into the pan and tap two times on the counter to get rid of the major air bubbles. Place the cake in the preheated oven and set the timer for 30 minutes. After 30 minutes, rotate the cake and set the timer for 15 more minutes. Check to see if the cake is baked through by quickly inserting a toothpick into the center of the cake and removing it to see if there is wet batter attached to the toothpick.

After it is finished baking, remove the cake from the oven and let it cool for 10 minutes on a wire rack. After 10 minutes, run a knife along the edge of the cake to loosen it from the sides of the pan. Release the springform or flip the cake out onto a parchment-lined cooling rack and then flip the cake back, right side up onto another parchment-lined cooling rack. Leave the cake to cool for at least 30 minutes before wrapping it up and putting it in the refrigerator to chill.

(continued)

**Raspberry Ice Cream
Layer**

1 batch of Raspberry Ice Cream
(page 143)

Once the cake has chilled, take it out of the refrigerator and use a long serrated knife to cut it into two equal layers. The top of the cake can be a little sticky on your hand, so I recommend laying a sheet of parchment paper or plastic wrap on the top of the cake while cutting it.

For the cleanest lines, use an adjustable cake collar or acetate collar to assemble. On a plate or small tray that will fit in your freezer, lay down a sheet of plastic wrap. Place the bottom layer of cake onto the lined plate with the cut side face up; wrap the collar around the chocolate cake so that it is snug around the cake but not squishing it, as it will then be difficult to fit the top layer in.

Raspberry Ice Cream Layer

Take the raspberry ice cream out of the freezer, let it defrost for 5 to 10 minutes, and then scoop it into a mixing bowl. Either by hand or with the paddle attachment on a stand mixer, stir the ice cream so that it becomes an even spreadable texture. Don't let it melt too much or the ice cream will run down the sides of the cake.

Pour the ice cream onto the bottom layer of cake. Use a rubber spatula to evenly spread it out and then place the top layer of cake over it with the cut side face down. Press down on the top layer of cake so that it lies level and firmly on the ice cream. Immediately place the cake back in the freezer overnight to refreeze.

Once frozen, take the cake out of the freezer and peel away the collar. If using a reusable collar, let it sit for 5 minutes before removing it. Dust the top with cocoa powder just before serving.

Let the cake sit for 10 to 15 minutes before slicing it with a long thin knife. It is best if you run the knife under hot water between each slice because it will both clean the knife and heat it up, making it easier to cut through the frozen cake. Wrap leftovers in plastic wrap and place them back in the freezer for next time!

Notes

The great part about this cake is that it can be made with any ice cream or even with a few different ones. If you have ice cream leftovers in your freezer, make half the cake one flavor and half another. Or get wild and swirl the ice creams together!

You can also dust the top with powdered sugar instead of cocoa powder if you prefer.

BLACKBERRY POPPYSEED CAKE | Brombeer Mohntorte

I saw a version of this cake on my last trip to Germany and knew I had to re-create it. The original was made with a cassis layer on top, which is a black currant liqueur, but for a light and alcohol-free version, I thought blackberries would be the perfect alternative. One of my favorite parts about many German cakes are the fruit layers made with fresh, seasonal fruit. They add so much flavor and brightness to the overall cake and create the perfect combination of textures.

This cake is relatively simple with just two layers—the base is a thick poppyseed cake with a hint of lemon and the top layer is pureed blackberries, set with gelatin and brightened with a little lemon juice. This cake can be made at any time of the year, but something about it just screams spring and summer to me.

Active Time: 2 hours

Total Time: 26 hours

Poppyseed Cake

144 g (½ cup + 1 tbsp + 2 tsp) butter

125 g (1 cup) all-purpose flour

50 g (¼ cup + 2 tbsp) cornstarch

1 tsp baking powder

4 large eggs, room temperature

1 medium lemon, zested

185 g (¾ cup + 2 tbsp) sugar

¼ tsp salt

45 g (⅓ cup) poppyseeds

Poppyseed Cake

Preheat the oven to 350°F (177°C) and place a rack in the center of the oven. Melt the butter in the microwave in short bursts or in a sauce pot on the stove. Set the melted butter aside. Sift the flour, cornstarch and baking powder together in a small bowl.

In the bowl of stand mixer, crack in all four eggs and add in the lemon zest, sugar and salt. Using the whisk attachment, mix on high until the mixture is very light and frothy—this should take 3 to 5 minutes and the eggs should be butter-colored. Turn the mixer down to medium-low speed and slowly stream the melted butter into the egg mixture, pouring it down the side of the bowl so that it doesn't hit the whisk while the mixer is running. Mix until everything is just combined.

Pour the sifted dry ingredients into the bowl and use the whisk attachment by hand to gently fold the dry ingredients in. This should be more of a folding motion, not stirring. Once the flour is almost completely mixed in, pour in the poppyseeds and repeat the same mixing process. If necessary, use a rubber spatula to finish mixing and scrape the bottom and sides of the bowl.

Line a 9-inch (23-cm) springform pan (a 9-inch [23-cm] metal cake pan will work too) with a baking spray that includes flour—just be sure to not overspray it or let much come up the sides of the pan. Alternatively, you can lightly grease the base with butter and then lay a circle of parchment paper on top. Pour the cake batter into the pan, tap twice on the counter to level it out and then place the cake in the preheated oven. Set the timer for 20 minutes.

After 20 minutes have passed, rotate the pan 180 degrees and bake for another 10 to 15 minutes, until the cake is golden brown and a toothpick inserted in the center of the cake comes out clean. Once baked, remove the cake from the oven and place on a wire rack to cool for at least 10 to 15 minutes. Then, run a knife along the edge, between the cake and the pan, to make sure that it didn't stick anywhere and then release the springform.

Leave the cake to cool fully to room temperature and then wrap it in plastic and store it in the refrigerator until it is cold and you are ready to assemble the cake.

(continued)

Blackberry Layer

225 ml (¾ cup + 3 tbsp) water, divided

14 g (1 tbsp + 1½ tsp) powdered gelatin (2 packets)

750 g (5 cups) frozen blackberries (or mixed berries), defrosted

50 g (¼ cup) sugar

15 ml (1 tbsp) lemon juice

50–75 g (3–5 tbsp) berry jam

Blackberry Layer

In a large bowl, add in 100 milliliters (¼ cup + 1½ tbsp) of cold water and sprinkle over the 14 grams (1 tbsp + 1½ tsp) of gelatin. Stir to combine and set aside. Pour the defrosted blackberries with 125 milliliters (½ cup + 1 tsp) of the water into a high-powered blender. Blend until smooth. Pour the blended mixture into a sauce pot and add in the sugar and lemon juice. Heat until the mixture is bubbling, stirring regularly to keep it from burning.

Once bubbles start to appear (this should take about 10 minutes), turn the heat off and pour the blackberry mixture into the bowl with the bloomed gelatin. Stir the gelatin into the blackberry mixture using a rubber spatula.

If you aren't in a hurry, the bowl can sit at room temperature with you stirring every 10 to 15 minutes so that the mixture cools evenly and no clumps form. If you want to move the process along, create an ice bath by placing the bowl into a larger baking dish with tall sides and adding ice and water into the baking dish around the bowl. This means you will need to stir the mixture frequently, but it will also cool down much faster.

Using a long serrated knife, cut off the top of the poppyseed cake so that the top is level and flat with the top edge of the sides. Find a plate or tray that is larger than the cake and lay a sheet of plastic wrap on it. Lay the cake, with the trimmed side facing up, on the sheet of plastic. Tape an acetate sheet/collar around the cake nice and tight. If you have an adjustable cake collar, I recommend still using acetate within it and then having the collar to reinforce it.

Spread the jam over the surface of the cake all the way to the edges, this will help seal any gap between the cake and acetate. Wrap the edges of the plastic wrap up around the acetate or cake collar. Place the cake on a shelf in your refrigerator. Once the blackberry mixture is fully cooled, use a small ladle to carefully pour the blackberry mixture over the jam layer. Leave the cake to set, in the refrigerator, for at least 24 hours. Once set, carefully peel the acetate collar off the cake. Use a long sharp knife to cut the cake into 8 or 12 slices depending on preference and clean the knife between each slice.

Note

This cake is best stored in the refrigerator so it isn't great for transporting long distances. If you do need to bring it somewhere, leave the cake collar on for stabilization until you arrive at your destination and then peel it off. Don't worry if some of the blackberry topping runs down, it will still be beautiful and delicious!

FRESH RASPBERRY & VANILLA CREAM CAKE | Himbeerkuchen

Servings: 8–12

This raspberry and vanilla cream cake is without a doubt one of my favorites. I once made it and gave it to my best friend, and she asked if I could make it for her wedding one day because she loved it so much. It's just the perfect combo of cake, cream and fruit.

Whenever I'm in Germany this is my go-to cake. It's light and fluffy but still creamy and refreshing. *Himbeerkuchen* is made in many different ways depending on which region in Germany you are in, but this recipe is made with a vanilla sponge cake, then a layer of vanilla Bavarian cream and finally, fresh raspberries with a raspberry gel. It's truly the perfect summer cake.

This recipe has quite a few steps, but it isn't difficult to follow, so don't be intimidated by the instructions. Work one section at a time and one step at a time and you will be so happy you did.

Active Time: 2 hours
Total Time: 2–3 days

Vanilla Cake

3 large eggs, room temperature

150 g (¾ cup) granulated sugar

¼ tsp salt

1 tsp vanilla extract

100 g (¾ cup + 2 tsp) all-purpose flour

50 g (¼ cup + 2 tbsp) cornstarch

1 tsp baking powder

100 ml (¼ cup + 2 tbsp) neutral oil (such as vegetable oil)

100 ml (¼ cup + 2 tbsp) water

Vanilla Cake

Preheat the oven to 350°F (177°C) and place a rack in the center of the oven. In the bowl of a stand mixer, add in the eggs, sugar, salt and vanilla. Whisk on high with the whisk attachment for 5 minutes, until the mixture is light and fluffy and lines begin to form as the whisk passes through. While the mixer is running, sift together the flour, cornstarch and baking powder into a small bowl. Turn the mixer down to medium-low speed and stream the oil and water down the inside of the bowl. Continue to whisk until the mixture is just combined.

Remove the bowl from the mixer and dump in the sifted dry ingredients. Hold the whisk attachment from the mixer in your hand and use it in a scooping and folding motion to mix the dry ingredients into the wet. Continue to mix until all the ingredients are combined and use a rubber spatula for the sides and bottom of the bowl if necessary.

Line a 9-inch (23-cm) springform pan (a 9-inch [23-cm] metal cake pan will work too) with a baking spray that includes flour—just be sure to not overspray it or let much come up the sides of the pan. Alternatively, you can lightly grease the base with butter and then lay a circle of parchment paper on top. Pour the cake batter into the pan and place the cake in the preheated oven. Set the timer for 20 minutes. After 20 minutes have passed, check to see if it is golden brown and a toothpick inserted in the center comes out clean. Another way to tell if it is done baking is to look and see if the edges of the cake are pulling away from the pan. If not, bake for 5 more minutes.

Once baked, remove the cake from the oven and place it on a wire rack to cool for at least 10 to 15 minutes.

Run a knife along the edge between the cake and the pan to make sure that it didn't stick anywhere and then release the springform. Leave the cake to cool fully to room temperature. Wrap the cake in plastic wrap and refrigerate until cold.

(continued)

Bavarian Cream Layer

200 ml (¾ cup + 1 tbsp + 1 tsp) milk, divided

7–8 g (2 tsp) powdered gelatin (1 packet)

3 egg yolks

25 g (2 tbsp) granulated sugar

1 tsp vanilla extract

200 ml (¾ cup + 1 tbsp + 1 tsp) heavy whipping cream, cold

500–600 g (4–4¾ cups) fresh raspberries

Bavarian Cream Layer

In a large heat-safe mixing bowl, add in 50 milliliters (3 tbsp + 1 tsp) of the milk and sprinkle the powdered gelatin over the top. Stir to combine, place a fine mesh sieve over the top of the bowl, and then set aside. In a medium heavy-bottomed sauce pot, add in the remaining 150 ml (½ cup and 2 tbsp) of milk. Turn the heat to medium and stir regularly until almost simmering. Just before the milk is simmering, add the egg yolks and sugar to a medium-sized bowl and whisk by hand to combine. Place the bowl on a damp towel or rag.

Once the milk is heavily steaming, turn off the heat and move the pot next to the bowl with the egg yolks. While whisking the egg yolks constantly with one hand, use a ladle in the other to gently and slowly pour more than half (at least 100 milliliters [⅓ cups + 1 tbsp]) of milk into the egg yolks. This is called tempering the eggs so they don't curdle. Now switch to whisking the remaining milk in the pot and pour in the tempered egg mixture. Return the pot to medium-low heat and switch to using a rubber spatula to stir the custard. Stir the custard in a figure eight motion and then once around the edge of the pot. Repeat this stirring motion until all of the bubbles from the surface have gone away and the mixture has thickened. This can take between 10 and 20 minutes.

Remove the pot from the heat and immediately pour the custard through the fine mesh sieve into the bowl with the bloomed gelatin. Remove the sieve and stir until the gelatin has fully dissolved and then whisk in the vanilla extract. Set the bowl aside to cool to room temperature—you will want to stir it and scrape the sides of the bowl often to keep it from clumping.

If you want to move the process along, create an ice bath by placing the bowl into a larger baking dish with tall sides and adding ice and water into the baking dish around the bowl. This means you will need to stir the mixture more frequently, but it will also cool down much faster. The mixture needs to be fully cooled but not stiff before folding in the whipped cream.

While the custard cools, set up the vanilla cake. Use a long serrated knife to level out the top of the cake. Place it on a parchment-lined tray or plate and wrap an acetate collar around it. It needs to be snug around the cake—an adjustable cake collar will work too. Wash the fresh raspberries and pat them dry.

Once the custard has cooled, use an electric mixer (stand or hand-held) to whip the cold cream on medium-high until medium peaks form. If you whip it to stiff peaks, it will be very difficult to fold smoothly into the custard. Pour the cooled custard into the whipped cream (if it isn't cooled, you will melt or even curdle the cream and have to start over). Use a wide, flat rubber spatula to fold the whipped cream into the custard until it is fully combined—it will be thick but runny. Use a ladle to carefully pour the custard on top of the vanilla cake. Spread it out into an even layer and make sure it touches all sides of the acetate to create a seal.

Carefully place it in the refrigerator for 20 to 30 minutes, until a light skin forms. Don't let it set fully, but just thick enough so that the raspberries don't sink in. Once it sets slightly, take the cake back out of the refrigerator and place the raspberries with the open side face down onto the Bavarian cream. Press down gently so that the raspberries are barely stuck into the cream. Drape a piece of plastic wrap over the acetate collar and put it in the refrigerator to set overnight.

Raspberry Layer

In a large bowl, add in 150 milliliters (½ cup + 2 tbsp) of the water and sprinkle the powdered gelatin over top. Stir to combine, place a fine mesh sieve over the top and set the gelatin mixture aside. In a large pot, add in the remaining 600 milliliters (2½ cups) of water, frozen raspberries and granulated sugar. Bring the mixture to a boil and mash the fruit until everything is broken up. Once hot, remove the pot from the heat and pour the fruit through the fine mesh sieve into the bowl with the bloomed gelatin. Remove the sieve and stir to combine.

Repeat the process of stirring the mixture until it is cooled as mentioned in the custard instructions. Use a rubber spatula to stir so the bubbles disappear. Leaving the cake in the refrigerator, use a ladle to carefully spoon the cooled but still liquid raspberry layer over the fresh raspberries. Don't worry if a couple raspberries pop up from the custard—it will still taste delicious. If there are any bubbles, try to pop them with a wooden or metal skewer as they won't disappear when it sets. Drape the plastic wrap back over the acetate collar but don't let it touch the raspberry liquid. Let the cake set overnight.

Take the cake out of the refrigerator and carefully peel the acetate collar away from the cake. Use a long, thin, sharp knife to cut the slices. Start by pressing the tip into the center of the cake and then pull the handle down through all the layers. Rinse off the knife between each cut to keep the layers and slices neat.

Raspberry Layer

750 ml (3 cups + 2 tbsp) water, divided

21 g (2 tbsp + 1 tsp) powdered gelatin (3 packets)

500 g (2 cups) frozen raspberries

100 g (½ cup) granulated sugar

Note

The raspberry gel can also be made with frozen strawberries if you can't find frozen raspberries. Or you can leave out the gel layer entirely and only top the cake with fresh raspberries, let the cream layer set completely, and enjoy!

VANILLA PUDDING APPLE CAKE |
Apfel Streuselkuchen mit Vanille Pudding

Makes: 8 slices

Vanilla pudding is such a key element to so many German sweets and this Vanilla Pudding Apple Cake is no different. A simple buttery shortcrust base, apple and vanilla pudding filling, all topped with buttery streusel, this cake is the perfect way to use up fresh apples in the fall.

If you've never had vanilla pudding baked into a cake, it might seem a bit unusual, but it goes so well with apples and thickens as it bakes to make a perfectly sweet and creamy apple filling. Plus, homemade vanilla pudding and German streusel are a match made in heaven, so I couldn't *not* include this cake.

Active Time: 1 hour

Total Time: 6–8 hours

Apples

4 medium apples (about 650 g)

Pudding

36 g (¼ cup + 1½ tsp) cornstarch

180 g (¾ cup + 2 tbsp) sugar

500 ml (2 cups + 1 tbsp + 1 tsp) milk

100 ml (⅓ cup + 1 tbsp + 1 tsp) heavy cream

40 g (3 tbsp) butter

10 ml (2 tsp) vanilla extract

Streusel

130 g (1 cup + ½ tbsp) all-purpose flour

85 g (⅓ cup + 1 tbsp) granulated sugar

93 g (⅓ cup + 1 tbsp + 1 tsp) butter, softened

1 tsp vanilla extract

Apples

Peel, quarter and core the apples. Cut the quarters into thin slices between ⅛ inch (8 mm) and ¼ inch (6 mm) in thickness. Put all the apples into a large heat-safe bowl.

Pudding

In a medium-sized sauce pot, whisk together the cornstarch and sugar. While whisking, slowly pour in the milk and then the heavy cream. Place the pot over medium heat and whisk constantly until the mixture thickens and lines from the whisk stay for about 1 second; this can take 5 to 15 minutes.

Once cooked, remove the mixture from the heat and add in the butter and vanilla extract. Whisk to combine. Pour the pudding into the bowl with the apples and stir to combine. Set the pudding-apple mixture aside to cool for 45 minutes to 1 hour while you prepare the streusel and crust. However, you do want to stir it occasionally to prevent the pudding from forming a skin.

Streusel

In a medium-sized bowl, whisk together the flour and sugar. Add in the softened butter and vanilla extract. Use a fork or your hands to rub the butter into the dry ingredients. Continue to mix until no dry bits remain and the mixture clumps easily.

(continued)

Crust

1 egg yolk

100 g (⅓ cup + 2½ tbsp) butter, softened

50 g (¼ cup) granulated sugar

1 tsp vanilla extract

175 g (1⅓ cups + 1 tbsp) all-purpose flour

1 tsp baking powder

¼ tsp kosher salt

Crust

Preheat the oven to 350°F (177°C) and place a rack in the center of the oven. In the bowl of a stand mixer, add in the egg yolk, butter, sugar and vanilla extract. Use the paddle attachment to cream the ingredients together for 2 minutes on medium speed. Scrape down the sides and bottom of the bowl. Pour in the flour, baking powder and salt, and mix again until the dough is just combined.

Line a 9 x 9–inch (23 x 23–cm) square metal pan by lightly greasing the bottom and two opposing sides of the pan. Cut a piece of parchment paper that is 9 x 15 inches (23 x 38 cm). Lay the piece of parchment paper onto the pan on the two sides and bottom of the pan that have been greased. Pour the dough into the lined pan. Gently press the dough into an even layer across the bottom of the pan. If the dough is too sticky to spread out by hand, put it in the refrigerator for 10 minutes and then continue to press the dough into the pan.

If the apple pudding mixture has cooled down, go ahead and move onto assembling. However, if it is still warm, place the crust in the refrigerator until the apple pudding mixture has cooled to room temperature or just barely warm.

Once cooled, pour the apple–vanilla pudding mixture into the pan with the crust. Crumble the streusel over the top. Place the assembled cake in the preheated oven and set the timer for 40 minutes. After 40 minutes, rotate the pan 180 degrees in the oven and bake for another 20 to 30 minutes. Once finished baking, the streusel should be golden brown.

Once baked, take the cake out of the oven and set it on a wire rack to cool for at least 45 minutes. After it has cooled to just a little warm to room temperature, place it in the refrigerator for at least 4 to 6 hours to set.

Take the cake out of the refrigerator and run a knife along the edges of the cake. Use the parchment paper to lift the cake out of the pan and place it on a cutting board. Use a long sharp knife to cut the cake in half in one direction. Turn the cake 90 degrees and cut the cake into fourths so that you are left with eight slices.

Notes

Cutting this cake can be a little difficult because of the crunchy streusel on top with the soft filling. If it makes you nervous, you can always cut the cake while it is still in the pan—it just isn't as good for your knives.

For serving, you can always top it with powdered sugar and sweetened whipped cream or leave it as-is.

Be sure to store leftovers in the refrigerator.

CHERRY STREUSEL CHEESECAKE | Kirsch Käsekuchen mit Streusel

Makes: 8–12 slices

Based on a classic German *Käsekuchen* made with *quark*, this cheesecake recipe is studded with tart cherries and topped with buttery streusel for a little extra flavor and texture. German cheesecake is different from American cheesecake for a couple of reasons: it uses quark and not cream cheese, which gives it a slightly lighter texture and it's baked, but not in a water bath, which does often lead to a little cracking but the texture stays smooth and creamy.

The bursts of tart cherries mixed with the rich and creamy cheesecake complement each other perfectly, but I could also see other berries being delicious in this cheesecake.

Active Time: 1 hour

Total Time: 12 hours

Crust

85 g (⅓ cup + 2 tsp) butter, softened

75 g (⅓ cup + 2 tsp) granulated sugar

1 tsp vanilla extract

1 large egg, room temperature

220 g (1¾ cups) all-purpose flour

½ tsp baking powder

Streusel

90 g (⅔ cup + 1 tbsp) all-purpose flour

60 g (¼ cup + 2 tsp) granulated sugar

60 g (¼ cup) butter, softened

1 tsp vanilla extract

Crust

Preheat the oven to 350°F (177°C) and place a rack in the center of the oven. In the bowl of a stand mixer, add in the butter, sugar and vanilla. Use the paddle attachment to beat the ingredients together on medium speed until all ingredients are combined. Add in the egg and mix again. Scrape down the sides of the bowl and then add in the flour and baking powder. Mix once more until no more dry ingredients are visible.

Pour the mixed crust into a 9-inch (23-cm) springform pan. First, press the crust into the bottom of the pan and then 2 inches (5 cm) up the sides. Be sure that the corner where the sides and bottom meet isn't too thick. You can do this by pressing the back of your pointer finger into the corner once the crust has been pressed into the whole pan. Place the crust in the refrigerator while preparing the rest.

Streusel

In a medium-sized bowl, whisk together the flour and sugar. Then, add in the butter and vanilla. Rub the butter into the dry ingredients using a fork, or your hands, until all of the butter has been fully mixed in.

(continued)

CHERRY STREUSEL CHEESECAKE |
Kirsch Käsekuchen mit Streusel (continued)

Cheesecake Filling

21 g (2 tbsp + 2 tsp) cornstarch

225 g (1 cup + 2 tbsp) granulated sugar

600 g (2¾ cups + 1½ tbsp) Quark, full fat (page 132)

100 g (⅓ cup + 1 tbsp + 1 tsp) sour cream

2 large eggs

10 ml (2 tsp) vanilla extract

150 g (1 cup) preserved tart cherries, drained

Cheesecake Filling

In a medium-sized mixing bowl, whisk together the cornstarch and granulated sugar. Then, add in the quark and stir to combine. Add in the sour cream, eggs and vanilla and whisk again until fully mixed.

Drain the tart cherries from a can or jar and measure out 150 grams (1 cup). Take the crust out of the refrigerator and pour the filling in. Sprinkle the cherries across the top and then crumble the streusel over top. Bake in the preheated oven for 40 minutes. After 40 minutes, rotate the pan 180 degrees and bake for another 30 to 40 minutes. You'll know it's done when you slightly shake the pan back and forth and it jiggles but doesn't look like the top is swimming around.

Once baked, take the cheesecake out of the oven and place it on a wire rack to cool to room temperature, for 1 to 2 hours. Once cooled, place it in the refrigerator for at least 6 hours to set. Remove the springform pan and use a long sharp knife to cut the chilled cheesecake into 8 to 12 slices. Optionally, dust the top with powdered sugar.

Note

This cheesecake keeps for quite a few days. I've kept mine for over a week, and it was still good. But, if you don't think you'll be able to finish it, slice the leftovers, wrap them in plastic wrap and store in resealable freezer bags in the freezer for a month or two. Thaw in the refrigerator overnight.

BAVARIAN PLUM CAKE | Zwetschgendatschi

Servings: 12

Zwetschgendatschi is a classic Bavarian sheet cake that is only available in mid- to late summer because it is made with *zwetschgen*, which are a very specific type of plum with a rather short growing season. But when zwetschgen are in season, you won't find a café without this delicacy. Zwetschgendatschi is usually made with either a yeasted dough or what is called a quark-oil dough. This recipe is made with the latter because I find it stays moist longer, whereas the yeasted dough has a tendency to dry out. If you are lucky enough to get your hands on zwetschgen, also known as prune plums (not dried) or Italian plums, PLEASE make this cake!

P.S. It's also delicious with a layer of buttery streusel on top like the one used for Streuseltaler (page 80) or drizzled with a little Vanille Soße (page 140).

Active Time: 45 minutes

Total Time: 1 hour 30 minutes

Cake Base

200 g (1½ cups + 2 tbsp) all-purpose flour

75 g (⅓ cup + 2 tsp) granulated sugar

1 tsp baking powder

1 large egg, room temperature

60 ml (¼ cup) neutral oil (such as vegetable oil)

100 g (½ cup) quark

1 tsp vanilla extract

Plum Topping

1.5 kg (3.3 lb) zwetschgen (approximately depending on the size of plums)

Cake Base

Preheat the oven to 350°F (177°C) and place a rack in the center of the oven. In the bowl of a stand mixer, whisk together the flour, sugar and baking powder. Then, add in the egg, oil, quark and vanilla extract. Use the dough hook to knead the dough for 10 to 15 minutes, until it is smooth. It can be a little sticky but not so sticky that you can't handle the dough without it all attaching to you.

Lightly grease the bottom of the pan with either soft butter or a baking spray with flour. Flip a 9 x 13–inch (23 x 33–cm) metal pan over and place the dough on the bottom. Gently roll the dough out so that it is almost the full size of the base of the pan. Lift the dough up, flip the pan back over, and lay the dough into the bottom of the pan. Stretch the edges of the dough to the edges of the pan and set aside.

Plum Topping

Rinse and pat the plums dry. Cut the plums into quarters, lengthwise and remove the stones. Lay the plum quarters with the skin side down onto the dough at a slight angle so that the back end of the quarter is sticking up higher than the other end. They should make a row across the pan on one short end. The edges of the plums should touch one another.

The next row will be almost exactly the same, but the slices should stagger the previous row so that the tips of these plums fit in the openings between the plums of the previous row. Repeat this until the whole pan is covered. Bake the cake in the preheated oven for 30 minutes. After 30 minutes, rotate the cake 180 degrees and bake for another 15 minutes.

Once baked, remove the cake from the oven and place on a wire rack to cool. After 15 to 20 minutes, carefully use a spatula to loosen the cake and slide it out onto a cutting board. Allow it to cool completely to room temperature before cutting it into nine squares measuring approximately 3 x 3 inches (8 x 8 cm).

Notes

If you can't find quark at your grocery store, there is a super simple recipe in this book on page 132 or you can use 5% fat Greek yogurt.

Unlike most recipes, I don't recommend swapping out these plums for a different plum if you can't find zwetschgen. I have tried it with other plums but they hold much more moisture and will create a very soggy cake.

VANILLA CREAM CAKE | Sahnetorte

Sahnetorte is essentially two layers of vanilla sponge cake, filled with a THICK layer of sweetened whipped cream and topped with a dusting of powdered sugar. The key to keeping this cake from being overly sweet or rich is the addition of quark in the filling because it has the right amount of tang to just cut through the cream filling. It's light, it's fluffy and above all else, it's creamy.

It may look basic, but the flavors and textures of this Sahnetorte are anything but. I love the versatility of this cake because it truly can work at any time of the year and for any occasion. Having friends over for an afternoon *kaffee*? Make this Sahnetorte the day before, and everyone will be oohing and awing. Need a birthday cake but don't want a big and heavy, overly sweet one? Make this Sahnetorte.

Active Time: 1 hour

Total Time: 24 hours

Vanilla Cake

3 large eggs, room temperature

150 g (¾ cup) granulated sugar

¼ tsp salt

1 tsp vanilla extract

100 g (¾ cup + 1 tbsp) all-purpose flour

50 g (¼ cup + 2 tbsp) cornstarch

1 tsp baking powder

100 ml (⅓ cup + 1 tbsp + 1 tsp) neutral oil (such as vegetable oil)

100 ml (⅓ cup + 1 tbsp + 1 tsp) water

Vanilla Cake

Preheat the oven to 350°F (177°C) and place a rack in the center of the oven. In the bowl of a stand mixer, add in the eggs, sugar, salt and vanilla. Whisk on high with the whisk attachment for 3 to 5 minutes, until the mixture is light and fluffy and lines begin to form as the whisk passes through. While the mixer is running, sift together the flour, cornstarch and baking powder into a small bowl. Turn the mixer down to medium-low speed and stream the oil and water down the inside of the bowl. Continue to whisk until everything is just combined.

Remove the bowl from the mixer and dump in the sifted dry ingredients. Hold the whisk attachment from the mixer in your hand and use it in a scooping and folding motion to mix the dry ingredients into the wet. Continue to mix until all ingredients are combined and use a rubber spatula for the sides and bottom of the bowl if necessary. Line a 9-inch (23-cm) springform pan (a 9-inch [23-cm] metal cake pan will work too) with a baking spray that includes flour—just be sure to not overspray it or let much come up the sides of the pan. Alternatively, you can lightly grease the base with butter and then lay a circle of parchment paper on top.

Pour the cake batter into the pan and place the cake in the preheated oven. Set the timer for 20 minutes. After 20 minutes have passed, check to see if it is golden brown and a toothpick inserted in the center comes out clean. Another way to tell if it is done baking is to look and see if the edges of the cake are pulling away from the pan. If not, bake for 5 more minutes.

Once baked, remove the cake from the oven and place it on a wire rack to cool for at least 10 to 15 minutes. Run a knife along the edge, between the cake and the pan, to make sure that it didn't stick anywhere and then release the springform. Leave the cake to cool fully to room temperature. Wrap it in plastic wrap and refrigerate until cold.

(continued)

Cream Filling

125 ml (½ cup + 1 tsp) milk, divided

7–8 g (2 tsp) powdered gelatin (1 packet)

100 g (½ cup) granulated sugar

500 g (2¼ cups + 2 tbsp) quark, low fat or full fat

400 ml (1⅔ cups) heavy whipping cream, cold

75 g (½ cup + 2 tbsp) powdered sugar, plus more for dusting

1 tsp vanilla extract

Notes

If you can't find quark at your grocery store, there is a super simple recipe in this book on page 132.

This cake is best eaten within 3 to 4 days and can be served as-is or with fresh fruit on top!

Cream Filling

In a large heat-safe mixing bowl, add in 50 milliliters (3 tbsp + 1 tsp) of the milk and sprinkle the powdered gelatin over the top. Stir to combine and set aside. In a small sauce pot, pour in the remaining 75 milliliters (¼ cup + 1 tbsp) of milk and 100 grams (½ cup) of granulated sugar. Heat on medium for 5 minutes, stirring frequently until the mixture is heavily steaming or just starting to simmer.

Once hot, remove the pot from the heat and pour the milk and sugar over the bloomed gelatin. Whisk together until all of the gelatin has melted. Pour the cold quark into the bowl with the milk and gelatin and whisk to combine. Allow the mixture to come to room temperature, whisking every 5 to 10 minutes, for about 30 minutes, before moving on to the next step.

While the quark cream cools, set up the vanilla cake. Use a long serrated knife to split the cake into two equal layers. Place the bottom layer on a parchment-lined tray or plate and wrap an acetate collar around it. It needs to be snug around the cake—an adjustable cake collar will work too. Once the quark cream has cooled, pour the cold heavy cream into the bowl of a stand mixer with the powdered sugar and vanilla extract. Use the whisk attachment to whip the cream, first on low until the powdered sugar has mixed in, and then on medium-high for 5 minutes, or until stiff peaks form, but don't walk away, or you'll be left with over-whipped cream, a.k.a. butter.

Add half of the whipped cream into the bowl with the quark cream. Use a wide, flat rubber spatula to fold the whipped cream in until fully combined. Add the second half of the whipped cream in and repeat the folding process until the creams are completely combined. Use a ladle to carefully pour the mixture on top of the vanilla cake. Spread it out into an even layer all the way to the collar edges. Place the top layer of the cake, cut side down, onto the cream filling. Press down gently to ensure no big air bubbles and to level out the cake. Chill the assembled cake in the refrigerator overnight.

The next day, take the cake out of the refrigerator and gently peel away the acetate collar. Transfer the cake to the desired serving dish and dust with a thin layer of powdered sugar.

Use a long, thin, sharp knife to cut the layers. I find it easiest to cut with the blade parallel with the top of the cake and gently slice through the top cake layer. Then, press the tip down in the center of the cake and bring the handle down after to cut through the cream and then the second cake layer. Clean the knife blade in between each slice.

POPPYSEED CHEESECAKE |
Mohn Käsekuchen

Servings: 8—12

Poppyseeds are very common in German recipes, and not just sprinkled in but used for their flavor as fillings. This recipe celebrates the poppyseed flavor with a thick layer of them cooked with milk, sugar and semolina, spread between the crust and the quark cheesecake filling.

When it comes to poppyseeds, the flavor can be somewhat polarizing, especially if you're new to them. However, with this cheesecake, because you get a bite of the creamy cheesecake filling and a bite of the buttery crust, the poppyseeds aren't as overwhelming. Plus, the golden brown, caramelized edges around the top that are typical in most German cheesecakes pair so well with the nutty poppyseed filling.

Active Time: 1 hour
Total Time: 12 hours

Crust

85 g (⅓ cup + 2 tsp) butter, softened

75 g (⅓ cup + 2 tsp) granulated sugar

1 tsp vanilla extract

1 large egg, room temperature

220 g (1¾ cups) all-purpose flour

1 tsp baking powder

Poppyseed Layer

250 ml (1 cup + 2 tsp) milk

75 g (⅓ cup + 2 tsp) granulated sugar

150 g (1 cup + 2 tsp) poppyseeds, ground

30 g (2 tbsp + 2 tsp) semolina flour

1 lemon, zested

Crust

Preheat the oven to 350°F (177°C) and place a rack in the center of the oven. In the bowl of a stand mixer, add in the butter, sugar and vanilla extract. Use the paddle attachment to cream the ingredients together for 2 minutes on medium speed. Scrape down the sides and bottom of the bowl. Add in the egg and mix again, but don't worry if it isn't completely smooth as this can happen if the egg is a little cold. Scrape down the bowl as necessary to ensure everything is mixed together.

Pour in the flour and baking powder and mix again until just combined. Line a 9-inch (23-cm) springform pan by greasing the bottom with soft or melted butter and then lay a circle of parchment paper on the bottom. Tip the crust into the lined pan. Gently press the crust into the bottom of the pan and then up the sides. The crust should be relatively thin everywhere. If it is too sticky to spread out by hand, put it in the refrigerator for 10 minutes and then continue to press the crust into the pan.

The crust should go about 2 inches (5 cm) up the side of the pan but don't worry too much about it being completely smooth and even. Once spread out, use the back of your pointer finger to press into the corners to ensure it isn't too thick—the corner where the sides and bottom meet should be the same thickness as the bottom and sides. Place the pan in the refrigerator while you make the Poppyseed Layer.

Poppyseed Layer

In a small sauce pot, add in the milk, sugar and ground poppyseeds. Heat over medium heat, stirring frequently until bubbling. While stirring constantly, pour in the semolina flour. Continue to cook and stir for about 10 minutes, until the mixture is thick. Once thick, remove the pot from the heat and add in the lemon zest. Pour into a large shallow dish and allow it to cool for 20 minutes while preparing the cheesecake.

(continued)

Cheesecake Layer

175 g (¾ cup + 1½ tbsp) granulated sugar

16 g (2 tbsp) cornstarch

600 g (2¾ cups + 1½ tbsp) full-fat quark

2 large eggs, room temperature

10 ml (2 tsp) vanilla extract

150 ml (½ cup + 2 tbsp) heavy cream

Cheesecake Layer

In a large mixing bowl, whisk the sugar and cornstarch together. Pour in the quark and stir to combine. Add in both eggs, vanilla and heavy cream and whisk again until smooth.

Take the crust out of the refrigerator and pour the poppyseed filling into the crust and smooth it out across the bottom. If it has become stiff, just do your best with your hands and spatula to make a smooth layer. Gently and slowly pour the cheesecake filling over the poppyseeds, being sure not to pour too fast and therefore breaking the poppyseed layer. Don't worry if the filling goes higher than the crust—it won't run down the sides during baking.

Place the assembled cheesecake in the preheated oven and set the timer for 40 minutes. After 40 minutes, rotate the pan 180 degrees in the oven and bake for another 20 minutes. Once finished baking, the cheesecake should still have a wobble but not seem soupy if jiggled. If needed, bake for another 10 minutes.

Once baked, take the cheesecake out of the oven and set it on a wire rack to cool for at least 20 minutes. Run a knife along the edge between the cake and the pan, then release the springform and leave it to cool to room temperature for 1 to 2 hours before placing it in the refrigerator for at least 6 hours to set. Once set, slice the cake with a long, thin, sharp knife, being sure to clean the blade between each slice.

Notes

If you can't find quark at your grocery store, there is a super simple recipe in this book on page 132. To grind the poppyseeds, I recommend using a spice grinder or an old coffee bean grinder; just be sure to clean it out first.

This cake can also be frozen; I recommend cutting it into slices and wrapping each one in plastic wrap, and then putting all of the slices in a resealable freezer bag and storing for up to 2 months. To defrost, take out however many slices you want the night before and let them defrost in the refrigerator overnight.

CHEESECAKE PUFF PASTRY STRUDEL | Quarkstrudel

Quarkstrudel is like a cheesecake baked inside of either strudel dough or puff pastry. I tried both when I was developing this recipe and decided to go with puff pastry for ease, but also because I like the texture of the pastry a little more with this filling! Quarkstrudel can also be called *topfenstrudel*—they are the same, only *topfen* is a different name used for quark in other regions.

On my most recent trip back to Germany, I made it a mission to try every Quarkstrudel I saw. They are so often dry and crumbly instead of smooth and creamy, and I wanted to make sure I had tried as many versions as possible before settling in on what I thought would be best. While it can be considered more traditional for the filling to be a bit dry, I prefer it to have a smoother, cheesecake-like consistency.

Unlike many of the cakes in this chapter that produce large cakes, this Quarkstrudel is a relatively small-batch sweet with just one sheet of puff pastry and eight small servings or four larger ones, so it can feel more accessible to make for any occasion.

Active Time: 20 minutes

Total Time: 8 hours

8 g (1 tbsp) cornstarch

90 g (⅓ cup + 1 tbsp + 1 tsp) granulated sugar

300 g (1¼ cups + 3 tbsp) full-fat quark

1 egg yolk

1 tsp vanilla extract

1 (245-g [8.6-oz]) sheet of puff pastry

20 g (2½ tbsp) powdered sugar

Notes

If you can't find quark at your local grocery store, there is a simple recipe in this book for homemade quark on page 132.

I don't recommend freezing this, as puff pastry doesn't do as well frozen.

Preheat the oven to 350°F (177°C) and place a rack in the center of the oven. In a medium-sized bowl, whisk together the cornstarch and granulated sugar. Pour in the quark and stir to combine. Lastly, add in the egg yolk and vanilla extract and whisk until the ingredients are combined.

Defrost one sheet of puff pastry. Line a 9 x 5–inch (23 x 13–cm) loaf pan with a parchment paper sling. It should be 8 inches (20 cm) wide and 15 inches (38 cm) long. The parchment should go down one long side of the pan, across the bottom, and back up the other side. Cut the sheet of puff pastry into two pieces, one being two-thirds of the rectangle and the other being the remaining third. Roll the two-thirds portion out on a lightly floured surface until it measures approximately 10 x 9 inches (25 cm x 23 cm).

Lay the larger piece of puff pastry into the loaf pan with the 10-inch (25-cm) sides going parallel with the long sides of the pan. The pastry should come up about 2 inches (5 cm) on each of the long sides and just barely on the short sides. Pour the quark filling into the loaf pan—you may need someone to hold up the long sides of the puff pastry while you pour the filling in.

The second piece of puff pastry should be rolled out to approximately 9 x 5 inches (23 x 13 cm). Lay this piece of puff pastry on top. Dampen one finger and use it to draw a line across both long edges of this piece of puff pastry. Then fold over any excess puff pastry from the long sides. Place the assembled strudel in the preheated oven for 30 minutes. After 30 minutes have passed, rotate the strudel pan 180 degrees and bake for another 15 minutes, until the puff pastry is golden brown.

Once baked, remove the pan from the oven and place it on a wire rack to cool to room temperature. Then, place the pan in the refrigerator to set for at least 4 hours or up to overnight.

Once set and ready to serve, use the parchment paper to lift the strudel out of the pan. Remove the parchment and set the strudel on a cutting board. Dust the top with powdered sugar and then cut into approximately 1-inch (2.5-cm) slices.

SWEET DOUGHS & BREADS | Süßer Teig & Brot

One of the first recipes I worked on when I started baking was for *Johannisbeerschnecken* (page 67), one of my all-time favorite German pastries. I could remember how they smelled and tasted and knew the flavors of sweet buttery streusel with tart juicy red currants would bring back all those summer memories of going to the corner bakery in the morning and picking out my favorite treat. When I finally got the recipe right, something clicked, and I knew from then on I would be able to re-create my favorites.

This chapter is full of pastries like Johannisbeerschnecken (page 67), Bavarian Style Donuts (page 79) and some of my favorite sweet breads! If you like sweet and fluffy dough filled with anything and everything from chocolate to fruit to poppyseeds, this chapter is meant for you. This is essentially what you would find at a German bakery and more! If you're not sure where to start, you can't go wrong with the *Vanille Stangen* (page 69)—bake them or fry them, they're delicious either way. I hope you love these recipes as much as I do!

RED CURRANT BUNS |
Johannisbeerschnecken

I don't like to play favorites, but if I had to pick a favorite from this chapter, it would be these *Johanisbeerschnecken*. Sometimes they're rolled like a cinnamon roll, which is how this recipe is made, and sometimes they're made more in the style of a Streuseltaler (page 80), but either way they're the perfect mix of sweet, enriched dough, tart red currants and buttery streusel.

One of the few *schnecken* recipes made without a laminated dough, these red currant pastries are similar to cinnamon rolls: they both have a yeasted dough, but these schnecken are filled with a vanilla custard pudding and red currants instead of butter and cinnamon sugar. The custard filling gives them a really fluffy and soft texture as it absorbs into the dough, not to mention the lemon glaze which enhances all of the flavors inside.

Active Time: 1 hour

Total Time: 3 hours

Dough

350 g (2¾ cups + 1 tbsp) all-purpose flour

50 g (¼ cup) granulated sugar

12 g (1 tbsp) instant yeast (1½ packets)

150 ml (½ cup + 2 tbsp) milk, lukewarm

80 g (⅓ cup + 1 tsp) butter, softened

1 large egg, room temperature

1 tsp vanilla extract

1 lemon, zested

Filling

10 g (1 tbsp + 1 tsp) cornstarch

25 g (1 tbsp + 2 tsp) granulated sugar

115 ml (⅓ cup + 2 tbsp + 1 tsp) milk

1 egg yolk

1 tsp vanilla extract

200 g (1¾ cups + ½ tbsp) frozen red currants, divided

Dough

In the bowl of a stand mixer, add in the flour, sugar and yeast. Whisk to combine and then add in the milk, butter, egg, vanilla extract and lemon zest. Use the dough hook attachment to knead on medium-low for 10 to 15 minutes, until the dough is smooth and the sides of the bowl are clean. Shape the dough into a ball and place in a lightly greased bowl (can be the same mixing bowl). Cover the bowl with a lid or plastic and place it somewhere warm to rise for 45 minutes, or until it is doubled in size. While the dough is rising, make the filling.

Filling

In a small sauce pot, whisk together the cornstarch and granulated sugar. Slowly pour in the milk while whisking constantly and then whisk in the egg yolk. Cook over medium-low heat for 5 to 10 minutes, whisking constantly until it thickens. Remove the mixture from the heat and whisk in the vanilla extract. Pour into a large shallow dish, lay a sheet of plastic wrap on the surface and allow it to cool while the dough proofs. Defrost the red currants.

(continued)

Streusel

60 g (½ cup) all-purpose flour

38 g (2½ tbsp) granulated sugar

38 g (2 tbsp + 2 tsp) butter, softened

1 tsp vanilla extract

Lemon Glaze

200 g (1⅔ cups) powdered sugar

45 ml (3 tbsp) lemon juice

Streusel

Whisk the flour and sugar together in a small mixing bowl and then add in the soft butter and vanilla. Use a fork or your fingers to rub the butter into the dry ingredients until it is fully mixed.

Preheat the oven to 350°F (177°C) and place two racks in the oven so they divide it into thirds. Line two baking sheets with parchment paper or silicone baking mats. Once doubled in size, knock the air out of the dough. Roll it out on a lightly floured surface to 10 x 16 inches (25 x 40 cm) and spread the custard filling over the dough, leaving a ½-inch (1.3-cm) border on all edges except one short side.

Sprinkle two-thirds of the defrosted red currants over the filling. Starting with the short side with no border and roll the dough up. It should be tight, but not so tight that the filling squeezes out. Use a ruler and a knife to make 1-inch (2.5-cm) marks across the top of the roll. Use a thin sharp knife to slice through the roll. Use a slicing motion to cut—don't just press down or the filling will squeeze out.

Place five to six rolls on each baking sheet and tuck the ends under the roll. Gently press down on each roll so they are about ¾ inch (2 cm) tall. Evenly divide and sprinkle the streusel over the top of each roll and press down again. Sprinkle the remaining red currants over the top of the streusel.

Leave the rolls to proof for 30 to 45 minutes, until they are puffy and jiggly. Once proofed, bake the schnecken in the preheated oven for 10 minutes. After the timer goes off, swap the pans and rotate 180 degrees. Bake for another 10 to 15 minutes, until they are golden brown.

Lemon Glaze

Whisk together the powdered sugar and lemon juice to make the glaze.

Once baked, take the pans out of the oven and leave them to cool on wire racks. While still warm, brush or drizzle each roll with the lemon glaze.

Note

These are great because they can be fully assembled the night before and baked in the morning. To do so, place them on baking sheets the night before, cover with a sheet of plastic wrap and put them in the refrigerator. In the morning, take them out and preheat the oven, allowing them to proof until they are puffy and jiggly—this will take a little longer since they have to warm up. Then, proceed with the baking instructions.

VANILLA TWISTS WITH VANILLA CREAM |
Vanille Stangen

Servings: 8

Soft yeasted dough, baked, rolled in butter and sugar and filled with a sweet vanilla cream, *Vanille Stangen* are so fun to make and even more fun to eat. You will find Vanille Stangen at most German *bäckereis* and for good reason. Sometimes they are filled with cream through the center and not cut open, but for the ultimate roll to filling ratio, I like to cut them open like a sandwich.

These are the ultimate sweet afternoon snack that you can pick up and eat while walking around or on your way home from school. Think of it as your afternoon PB&J but so much better. This recipe bakes the twists, but you can also fry them the way that the Lemon Raspberry Donuts (page 73) are fried and then omit the butter for rolling and roll them straight in the sugar! If you're usually a chocolate person and not sure about these, let me just say they put up quite the fight against some of my favorite chocolate sweets.

Active Time: 45 minutes

Total Time: 1 hour 45 minutes

Vanilla Cream

28 g (3½ tbsp) cornstarch

80 g (6 tbsp) granulated sugar

300 ml (1¼ cups) milk

2 egg yolks

1 tsp vanilla extract

200 ml (¾ cup + 1 tbsp + 1 tsp) heavy cream, cold

Dough

500 g (4 cups) all-purpose flour

50 g (¼ cup) sugar

15 g (1 tbsp + 1 tsp) instant yeast (2 packets)

250 ml (1 cup + 2 tsp) milk

1 large egg, room temperature

1 egg yolk

60 g (¼ cup + 1 tsp) butter, softened

1 tsp vanilla extract

Vanilla Cream

In a medium-sized sauce pot, whisk the cornstarch and sugar together. While whisking, slowly pour in the milk and whisk until combined and then whisk in both egg yolks. Place the pot over medium heat and whisk continuously for 10 to 15 minutes, until the mixture has thickened and bubbles at least once. You will be able to see the lines of the whisk in the pudding.

Once thickened, remove the pot from the heat and whisk in the vanilla extract. Pass the pudding through a fine mesh sieve into a large and shallow dish. Lay a sheet of plastic over the surface to prevent it from forming a skin and leave the pudding to cool to room temperature while preparing the rolls—it should be the right temperature when the rolls are finished.

Dough

In the bowl of a stand mixer, add in the flour, sugar and yeast. Then whisk it together. Add the milk, egg, egg yolk, butter and vanilla extract into the bowl and knead the mixture with the dough hook on the stand mixer for 10 to 15 minutes on low speed, until the dough is smooth and the bowl is clean. Remove the dough and shape it into a ball. Lightly grease the mixing bowl and place the ball of dough back in. Cover the bowl with a lid or plastic and place somewhere warm for 30 to 45 minutes. The dough should double in size.

Preheat the oven to 350°F (177°C). Arrange two racks so that they divide the oven into thirds and line two baking sheets with silicone mats or parchment paper. Divide the dough into 16 equal portions. Shape each portion into a flat oval about 4 inches (10 cm) long. Roll one of the long edges of the oval up to the other side to create a log. Pinch the seam and ends shut, then roll the log out to about 8 inches (20 cm) long.

(continued)

Sugar Coating

60 ml (¼ cup) butter, melted

200 g (1 cup) granulated sugar

Twist two of the logs together about three or four times and pinch the ends so that they don't unroll. Place four twists onto each baking sheet, leaving at least 3 inches (8 cm) between each roll. Drape a sheet of plastic over the rolls and leave them to rest for 30 minutes somewhere warm.

Once puffy and almost doubled in size, bake the twists in the preheated oven for 8 minutes. Swap and rotate the baking sheets 180 degrees and bake for another 7 minutes.

Sugar Coating

When the *stangen* are finished baking, work one at a time and brush them with the melted butter and then roll them in granulated sugar. Leave them to cool before assembling.

If the vanilla pudding is very stiff, use an electric whisk to beat it until smooth. Pour the cold heavy cream into the bowl of a stand mixer and use the whisk attachment to whisk on medium-high speed until stiff peaks form. Gently fold the stiff whipped cream into the vanilla pudding and fill it into a piping bag. Slice each baked roll in half like a hotdog bun. Pipe the vanilla cream filling onto the bottom of each roll and then press the top on the cream to make a cream sandwich and enjoy!

Notes

These are best when made and eaten on the same day, but they will keep ok in the refrigerator if stored in an airtight container for a couple days.

These can also be fried for a more classic donut texture. Follow the frying instructions on page 74 and fry one at a time for 1 minute and 30 seconds per side. I sometimes like to fry half while the other half is baking.

LEMON RASPBERRY DONUTS |
Zitronen Himbeer Krapfen

Servings: 12

These are the perfect summer donuts. Depending on where you are in Germany, these will be called anything from *krapfen* to *Berliner* to *kreppel* and more, but for now we'll just call them krapfen. Similar to donuts, krapfen are fried, enriched doughs (meaning there's eggs and butter added to the yeasted dough), and this recipe also has lemon zest in the dough, lemon juice in the glaze and fills them with yummy raspberry jam.

I love these donuts because they're so big and fluffy and they don't have to sit overnight. Plus, the lemon and raspberry add the perfect burst of flavor to these otherwise simple donuts. I rolled half in a lemon sugar and the other half in a lemon glaze—to do so, simply halve the amounts listed in the ingredients. If you find frying intimidating, I 100 percent understand, but I'm also here to be your frying fairy godmother and help you along the way and remind you that it gets easier the more you practice!

Active Time: 1 hour

Total Time: 2 hours

Dough

500 g (4 cups) all-purpose flour

50 g (¼ cup) granulated sugar

15 g (1 tbsp + 1 tsp) instant yeast (2 packets)

250 ml (1 cup + 2 tsp) milk, lukewarm

1 large egg, room temperature

1 egg yolk

60 g (¼ cup + 1 tsp) butter, softened

1 tsp vanilla extract

1 lemon, zested

Frying

2 L (67.6 fl oz) vegetable oil

Dough

In the bowl of a stand mixer, add in the flour, sugar and yeast; whisk to combine. Then, add in the milk, egg, egg yolk, butter, vanilla extract and lemon zest. Use the dough hook attachment to knead on medium-low for 15 to 20 minutes, until the dough is smooth and the sides of the bowl are clean.

Shape the dough into a ball and place it in a lightly greased bowl (can be the same mixing bowl). Cover the bowl with a lid or plastic and place somewhere warm to rise for 45 minutes, until it is puffy and doubled in size. While the dough rises, pour the oil into a Dutch oven or heavy-bottomed large pot. Place a thermometer into the oil and heat on medium-low until the oil reaches 350°F (177°C).

Place a wire rack onto a baking sheet and lay two layers of paper towels on top of the rack.

Prepare the topping of choice, lemon sugar or lemon glaze (or both!). For the lemon glaze, whisk the powdered sugar and lemon juice together until thin. For the lemon sugar, zest the lemon into a bowl with the sugar. Rub the lemon zest into the sugar with your fingers.

Once doubled in size, knock the air out of the dough and divide it into 12 equal portions. Shape each portion into a ball by first flattening it slightly into a disk and then tucking all the edges of the disk under. Shape your hand into a claw over the ball of dough with the smooth side face up. Roll the ball around in your hand on a clean work surface to create tension on the dough and seal the seam on the bottom of the ball. Refer to the process images in the Plum and Poppyseed Donuts (page 112) for shaping instructions.

Place the shaped rolls on a well-floured baking sheet or tray and drape a piece of plastic wrap over the top of the rolls to prevent them from drying out. Place them somewhere warm until they have grown to almost twice the size, look a bit puffy and the oil is hot.

(continued)

LEMON RASPBERRY DONUTS |
Zitronen Himbeer Krapfen (continued)

Topping

Lemon glaze: 150 g (1 cup + 3 tbsp) powdered sugar + 60 ml (4 tbsp) lemon juice

OR

Lemon sugar: 200 g (1 cup) zest of 1 lemon + granulated sugar

Filling

600 g (1¾ cups + 2 tbsp) raspberry jam

Frying

To fry the donuts, use a metal spatula or spider to lift three of the donuts from the floured sheet (one at a time) and slowly lower them into the hot oil. Fry for 1 minute and 30 seconds to 2 minutes on one side until they are golden brown. Use a metal spider to flip them and fry them again for 2 minutes. Use a spider or slotted spoon to lift them out of the hot oil and place them on the paper towel–lined cooling rack. Allow the oil to return to 350°F (177°C) if necessary and then add in three more donuts.

Topping

While the next batch is frying, dip each freshly fried donut in lemon glaze or roll in lemon sugar and place on a second wire rack to cool fully.

Filling

Once cooled to just warm, poke a hole in the side of each krapfen with the tip of a paring knife. Fit a piping bag with a metal tip and fill it with the raspberry jam (a ziplock bag with a hole cut into one of the bottom corners will work too). Place the tip of the bag in the hole of each donut and squeeze about 60 grams (3 tbsp) of raspberry jam into each one. Enjoy these fresh!

Note

It's important to pay attention to the dough because you don't want it to overproof at any step—you'll be able to tell because the surface of the dough will appear transparent and veiny. But you also don't want to underproof the dough because they won't be as light and airy as possible. This doesn't mean you have to sit there watching it the whole time. Just check on it every 10 to 15 minutes, until you get comfortable with it.

FRIED CINNAMON SUGAR APPLE ROLLS | Apfelschnecken

Servings: 11–12

There's just something about apples and cinnamon (sugar) that will just always make sense, no matter the application. but *especially* as a filling inside in fluffy yeasted, fried dough that is then rolled in cinnamon sugar. Think "cinnamon roll" but with apples and cinnamon flavor, and then fried like a donut—yeah, they're really good.

Apfelschnecken can be found at most bakeries in Germany alongside other baked schnecken and krapfen but let me tell you, they are well worth the effort to make fresh at home! They have such a fall donut feel about them, but really you can make them any time and you'll never regret it.

Active Time: 1 hour

Total Time: 2 hours 30 minutes

Dough

425 g (3¼ cups + 2 tbsp) all-purpose flour

100 g (½ cup) granulated sugar

15 g (1 tbsp + 1 tsp) instant yeast (2 packets)

175 ml (½ cup + 3 tbsp + 2 tsp) milk, lukewarm

1 large egg, room temperature

1 egg yolk

1 tsp vanilla extract

60 g (¼ cup + 1 tsp) butter, softened

Frying

2 L (67.6 fl oz) vegetable oil

Filling

1 large apple

Juice of ½ lemon (approximately 15 ml [1 tbsp])

Dough

In the bowl of a stand mixer, whisk together the flour, sugar and yeast. Pour in the lukewarm milk, egg, egg yolk, vanilla extract and butter. Use the dough hook attachment to knead the dough on medium-low speed until smooth and no longer sticking to the sides of the bowl. This should take 10 to 20 minutes but can take longer.

Shape the dough into a ball and place in a lightly greased bowl (can be the same mixing bowl). Cover the bowl with a lid or plastic wrap and set it somewhere warm to rest for 1 hour.

While the dough rests, heat the oil in a large, heavy-bottomed pot with a thermometer to 330°F (166°C), and prepare the apple for the filling.

Filling

Peel and core the large apple. Cut into pieces that are no more than ¼ inch (6 mm) thick, but they can be up to ½ inch (1.3 cm) long or wide. Put the chopped apple into a bowl and pour the lemon juice on top. Stir to combine and set aside.

Place a wire rack onto a baking sheet and lay two layers of paper towels on top of the rack—this is where the schnecken will go once they are fried.

Frying

Generously dust a baking sheet or tray with flour (you may need two or a tray and a plate).

Once doubled in size, knock the air out of the dough and roll it out on a lightly floured surface to approximately 11 x 17 inches (28 x 42 cm). Pour the apple chunks onto the dough. It's ok if a little lemon juice comes with them.

Evenly spread the apple bits over the dough; it won't seem like a lot, but it will be plenty. Make sure all apple chunks are lying down so that they aren't more than ¼ inch (6 mm) high. Starting at one short end, roll the dough up tightly, giving it a squeeze after every roll, until you reach the other short end. Pinch the end into the roll to create a sealed seam. Squeeze the roll gently all the way along to make sure everything is holding together. This will also lengthen the roll slightly.

(continued)

FRIED CINNAMON SUGAR APPLE ROLLS |
Apfelschnecken (continued)

Rolling

150 g (¾ cup) granulated sugar

5 g (2 tsp) ground cinnamon

Note

As with most fried recipes, these are best eaten fresh or the same day they are fried. Keep a close eye on the oil and don't let it change more than 5 degrees up or down. These are fried at a lower temperature to ensure the center is cooked without the outside getting too dark.

Place the roll seam side down and use a ruler and a knife to mark 1-inch (2.5-cm) slices on top of the roll. Once marked, slice through the roll with a slicing motion; don't just press down as you may need to cut through apple pieces. Place each slice onto the floured baking sheet or tray, making sure the end of the spiral is stuck to the roll. Leave them to proof for 20 to 30 minutes, until the oil is hot. In a medium bowl, stir together the cinnamon and sugar and set aside.

Once proofed, fry two schnecken at a time in the hot oil. Use a metal spatula, if necessary, to lift the schnecken off of the baking sheet and carefully lower them into the hot oil. Fry on each side for 1 minute and 30 seconds. Use a slotted spoon or metal spider to flip them over after the timer goes off and then fry again for another 1 minute and 30 seconds. Use that same slotted spoon or spider to lift the light golden brown schnecken out of the oil and place them on the paper towel–lined rack next to the pot to allow the oil to drip off. Make sure the oil heats back up to 330°F (166°C) if it has dropped before frying the next two.

Rolling

While the next batch is frying, roll the first batch in the cinnamon sugar and then place them on a wire rack or whichever dish you plan to serve them on. Continue frying and rolling until all are cooked.

BAVARIAN STYLE DONUTS | Ausgezogene

As kids, we would go every weekend with my dad to get fresh, fried donuts. I loved going in and smelling the sweet, fried dough and knowing that it meant that one of those donuts would soon find its way into my watering mouth. I think it's safe to say that's where my love of donuts started and it hasn't really stopped, so when I had *Ausgezogene* for the first time, I knew we needed a recipe.

Fluffy fried dough, pulled thin in the center and nice and pillowy on the edges, topped with powdered sugar or rolled in granulated sugar, these Bavarian-style donuts are so fun and different! Made with a simple doughnut dough, Ausgezogene are really just a fun way to shape donuts and make them soft and fluffy all the way around and thin and flat in the middle. They're sold at so many bakeries in Germany, and they're just so yummy.

Active Time: 1 hour

Total Time: 2 hours

---

500 g (4 cups) all-purpose flour

50 g (¼ cup) granulated sugar

15 g (1 tbsp + 1 tsp) instant yeast (2 packets)

250 ml (1 cup + 2 tsp) milk, lukewarm

1 large egg, room temperature

1 egg yolk

60 g (¼ cup + 1 tsp) butter, softened

1 tsp vanilla extract

2 L (67.6 fl oz) vegetable oil

50 g (¼ cup + 2 tbsp) powdered sugar for dusting, or 100 g (½ cup) granulated sugar for rolling

---

Note

It can take a few tries to get the shaping down, but most importantly don't let them sit for too long before shaping and frying because they will overproof and fall flat. If your oil is taking a long time to heat up, slow down the proofing by putting them in the refrigerator until you are ready.

In the bowl of a stand mixer, add in the flour, sugar and yeast. Whisk to combine. Add in the milk, egg, egg yolk, butter and vanilla extract. Use the dough hook attachment to knead on medium-low for 15 to 20 minutes, until the dough is smooth and the sides of the bowl are clean.

Shape the dough into a ball and place it in a lightly greased bowl (can be the same mixing bowl). Cover the bowl with a lid or plastic and place somewhere warm to rise for 45 minutes.

While the dough rises, pour the oil into a Dutch oven or large, heavy-bottomed pot. Place a thermometer into the oil and heat on medium-low until the oil reaches 350°F (177°C). Place a wire rack onto a baking sheet and lay two layers of paper towels on top of the rack.

Once doubled in size, knock the air out of the dough and divide it into 12 equal portions. Shape each portion into a ball by first flattening it slightly into a disk and then tucking all the edges of the disk under. Shape your hand into a claw over the ball of dough with the smooth side face up. Roll the ball around in your hand on a clean work surface to create tension on the dough and seal the seam on the bottom of the ball.

Using a rolling pin, barely flatten out each roll so that they are about 1½ inches (3.5 cm) thick. Place the gently flattened dough balls on a well-floured tray and cover for 20 to 30 minutes. Once puffy, slightly risen and the oil has reached 350°F (177°C), it's time to shape and fry. Working with one portion of dough at a time, pinch the center of the dough and stretch it until it is thin to the point that light can pass through. The center should be at least 1½ inches (4 cm) in diameter while leaving the edges puffy. Only press the centers into the two that you are frying at a time. Once the centers have been pressed in, gently lower each dough portion into the oil, allowing oil to run into the center dimple. If oil doesn't flow into the center, and rather the center puffs up, don't worry, it will work too!

Fry the Ausgezogene for 60 to 90 seconds on each side until they are golden brown. Use tongs or a metal spider to flip them and fry again for 60 to 90 seconds. Use a spider or slotted spoon to lift them out of the hot oil and place them on the paper towel–lined cooling rack. Repeat the pressing, stretching, frying and flipping for the remaining dough portions. While the next batch is frying, dust the freshly fried batch with powdered sugar or roll them in a bowl of granulated sugar. Serve still warm!

GLAZED STREUSEL PASTRIES | Streuseltaler   Servings: 12

Simple but delicious. One of my favorite parts of German sweets is the streusel, it's buttery, sweet, a little crunchy and basically tastes amazing on top of almost any pastry. These *Streuseltaler* are made with a fluffy, donut-like dough, brushed with just a little Quark (page 132), which prevents them from drying out, and topped with buttery streusel before being baked and then drizzled with a little lemon glaze.

These would also be delicious with a little jam spread onto the dough before sprinkling the streusel on for a little extra burst of flavor. And if you love these, you have to try the Johannisbeerschnecken (page 67) at the beginning of this chapter!

Active Time: 45 minutes

Total Time: 2 hours 20 minutes

Yeasted Dough

350 g (2¾ cups) all-purpose flour

100 g (½ cup) granulated sugar

12 g (1 tbsp) instant yeast (1½ packets)

150 ml (½ cup + 2 tbsp) milk, lukewarm

1 large egg, room temperature

100 g (¼ cup + 3 tbsp) butter, softened

1 lemon, zested

1 tsp vanilla extract

Streusel Layer

175 g (1¼ cups + 2 tbsp) all-purpose flour

125 g (½ cup + 1 tbsp+ 2 tsp) granulated sugar

125 g (½ cup + 1 tbsp) butter, softened

1 tsp vanilla extract

150 grams (¾ cup) quark

Dough

In the bowl of a stand mixer, add in the flour, sugar and yeast. Whisk to combine and then add in the milk, egg, butter, lemon zest and vanilla extract. Use the dough hook attachment to knead on medium-low for 10 to 15 minutes, until the dough is smooth and the sides of the bowl are clean.

Shape the dough into a ball and place in a lightly greased bowl (can be the same mixing bowl). Cover the bowl with a lid or plastic and place somewhere warm to rise for 45 minutes. Preheat the oven to 350°F (177°C) and arrange two racks so that they split the oven into thirds.

Streusel Layer

Whisk the flour and sugar together in a small mixing bowl and then add in the soft butter and vanilla. Use a fork or your fingers to rub the butter into the dry ingredients until it is fully mixed.

Line two baking sheets with parchment paper or silicone baking mats.

Once doubled in size, knock the air out of the dough and divide it into 12 equal portions. Shape each portion into a ball and then gently roll it out to 4 inches (10 cm) in diameter. Place six rounds of dough onto each lined baking sheet, evenly spaced. Cover with a kitchen towel or sheet of plastic wrap. Set aside somewhere warm and leave to proof for 30 minutes.

Spoon 13 grams (1 tbsp) of quark onto each round and use the back of a spoon to spread it out, leaving a ½-inch (12-mm) border around the edges. Crumble the streusel over top of each pastry. Place the assembled pastries in the preheated oven and set a timer for 10 minutes. After 10 minutes, swap the pans and rotate them 180 degrees. Bake for another 10 minutes, until they are golden brown.

Once baked, remove the baking sheets from the oven and place them on a wire rack to cool for at least 10 minutes. Top with either the lemon glaze from the *Mohnschnecken* recipe (page 101) or dust with powdered sugar.

Notes

If you can't find quark at your grocery store, there is a simple recipe for home-made quark on page 132.

These are best if eaten the day they are baked but can be stored in an airtight container for a day or two. They can also be frozen if wrapped up individually.

QUARK PUFF PASTRY HAND PIES |
Quarktaschen

Servings: 4

Directly translated, *Quarktaschen* means "quark pouches" or "purses," which is essentially what a hand pie is: a little pouch with filling! These are made with squares of puff pastry, filled with a quark mixture that makes a creamy, cheesecake-like, sweet center once baked, and then finished off with a generous dusting with powdered sugar.

I've also seen these made with a yeasted, laminated dough, like the one on page 87, but sometimes that feels like a lot. So, on days where laminated dough from scratch just isn't going to happen, we make these Quarktaschen because they're made with store-bought puff pastry (of course you can make your own if you prefer), which means all you really have to do is make the filling and assemble. They're much easier than they look, and it's worth it just to enjoy one of these perfect little pastry pouches.

Active Time: 20 minutes
Total Time: 1 hour

15 g (2 tbsp) cornstarch

50 g (¼ cup) granulated sugar

150 ml (½ cup + 2 tbsp) milk

150 g (¾ cup) full-fat quark, divided

1 egg yolk

1 tsp vanilla extract

1 (245-g [8.6-oz]) sheet of puff pastry, thawed

50 g (¼ cup + 2 tbsp) powdered sugar for dusting

Notes

If you can't find quark at your grocery store, there is a simple recipe for making homemade quark on page 132.

This recipe can be easily doubled or tripled depending on how many you want to make.

If you are making your own puff pastry, just make sure your sheet also weighs approximately 245 grams (8.6 oz).

In a medium-sized sauce pot, whisk the cornstarch and sugar together. While whisking, slowly pour in the milk. Add in half of the quark and egg yolk and whisk again. Cook over medium heat, whisking regularly until the mixture is thick and steaming. Remove from the heat and whisk in the remaining quark and vanilla extract.

Pour the quark filling into a large shallow dish and allow it to cool to room temperature or cover with a sheet of plastic wrap and place in the refrigerator until cold. Preheat the oven to 400°F (204°C) and place a rack in the center of the oven. Line a baking sheet with parchment paper.

Fill a small bowl with 30 milliliters (2 tbsp) of water. Roll the sheet of puff pastry out until it is thin, pliable and a square. It should be about ⅛ inch (6 mm) thick. Use a sharp knife to cut the pastry into four equal squares. Place the squares onto the lined baking sheet.

Spoon the cooled quark filling into the center of each pastry. Bring two opposite corners to the center, holding them high above the quark filling. Dab a little water onto one corner and press the other corner on top, overlapping them about ½ inch (1.3 cm). Dab the top corner with water and bring one of the remaining corners over top of the previous two and repeat with the last corner. Once all corners have been brought together, let go and allow them to fall on top of the filling.

Repeat this assembling process for the remaining three pastries.

Place the baking sheet with the pastries in the preheated oven for 10 minutes. After 10 minutes, rotate the pan 180 degrees and bake for another 5 to 10 minutes, until the pastries are golden brown.

Once baked, take the sheet out of the oven and place them on a wire rack to cool. Once cooled, dust them with powdered sugar.

LEMON POPPYSEED STREUSEL TWIST | Mohnstriezel

At this point you're probably thinking, another yeasted dough recipe with streusel on top? Yes, ok, but hear me out. Yeasted dough is truly one of the foundations of German baking, and you would be hard-pressed to walk into a German bakery and see it completely free of streusel. The magical part of these two elements is that they are so versatile and work with almost any flavor profile under the sun.

Similar to a *Mohnstrudel* or poppyseed strudel (page 101), this *Mohnstriezel* is made with a yeasted dough, rolled up with a creamy poppyseed filling, topped with buttery streusel and finished off with a little lemon glaze. If you aren't sure about poppyseeds, this recipe can be a great little introduction, because it highlights the poppyseeds without hitting you in the face with them.

Active Time: 1 hour

Total Time: 3 hours

Dough

250 g (2 cups) all-purpose flour

40 g (2 tbsp + 2 tsp) granulated sugar

8 g (2 tsp) instant yeast (1 packet)

125 ml (½ cup + 1 tsp) milk, lukewarm

40 ml (2 tbsp + 2 tsp) butter, melted

1 tsp vanilla extract

½ lemon, zested

Poppyseed Filling

75 g (½ cup + 1 tsp) poppyseeds

50 g (¼ cup) granulated sugar

175 ml (½ cup + 3 tbsp + 2 tsp) milk

35 g (3 tbsp) semolina

½ lemon, zested

Streusel

40 g (⅓ cup) all-purpose flour

30 g (2 tbsp) granulated sugar

30 g (1 tbsp) butter, softened

1 tsp vanilla extract

Dough

In the bowl of a stand mixer, add in the flour, sugar and yeast. Whisk to combine everything. Add in the milk, butter, vanilla extract and lemon zest. Use the dough hook attachment to knead on medium-low for 15 minutes. This dough is quite stiff, so turn the mixer down to low if necessary.

Shape the dough into a ball and place in a lightly greased bowl (can be the same mixing bowl). Cover the bowl with a lid or plastic and place it somewhere warm to rise for at least an hour. Because of how stiff this dough is, it can take a little longer to proof but be sure to let it grow and get puffy. Preheat the oven to 350°F (177°C) and place a rack in the center of the oven.

Poppyseed Filling

Blend the poppyseeds in a high-powered blender until they turn into more of a powder.

In a medium-sized sauce pot, add in the sugar and milk and stir to combine. Cook over medium heat for 5 to 10 minutes, stirring frequently until the mixture is bubbling. Slowly pour in the semolina, whisking constantly until starting to thicken and then pour in the poppyseeds. Continue to cook until thick, about 5 minutes.

Once cooked, remove the filling from the heat and stir in the lemon zest. Transfer to a shallow dish and set aside to cool until it is warm.

Streusel

Whisk the flour and sugar together in a small mixing bowl. Then, add in the softened butter and vanilla. Use a fork or your fingers to rub the butter into the dry ingredients until it is fully mixed in.

(continued)

Lemon Drizzle

100 g (¾ cup + 1 tbsp)
powdered sugar

2 tbsp (30 ml) lemon juice

Lemon Drizzle

Whisk the powdered sugar and lemon juice together into a thick drizzle.

Line a baking sheet with parchment paper or a silicone baking mat. Once puffy, knock the air out of the dough and roll it out on a lightly floured surface to 10 x 14 inches (25 x 35 cm).

Crumble the poppyseed filling evenly over the dough. Use your hands or a spatula to spread the filling into a flat and even layer, leaving a ½-inch (12-mm) border around all edges except 1 long side. Starting with the long side with no border, roll the dough up to the other long side. With the seam side down, cut the roll in half lengthwise with a long sharp knife.

Twist the two halves together four times, with the poppyseed filling face up and visible. Pinch the ends together and tuck them under the twist. Place the twist on the lined baking sheet. Press the streusel into the top of the twist. Drape the twist with plastic wrap or a kitchen towel and leave to proof for 45 minutes to 1 hour. It should have grown decently, but not necessarily doubled in size.

Once puffy, bake the twist for 30 minutes in the preheated oven. After the timer goes off, rotate the pan 180 degrees and bake for another 10 to 15 minutes. If it starts to look dark, cover the twist with a piece of aluminum foil.

Once baked and golden brown, take the twist out of the oven and place the baking sheet on a wire rack to cool fully. Drizzle the top of the twist with the lemon drizzle.

Notes

This dough is quite stiff, but that is what helps it keep its shape, so don't be tempted to add more liquid.

The streusel tends to insulate the inside of the *striezel*, so be sure to bake it for the full amount of time and don't pull it out when it is just barely golden brown.

LAMINATED DOUGH |
Plunderteig

This dough is the foundation for so many of my favorite pastries in this book. It is the type of dough often used for croissants, but don't let that intimidate you. Every step you need has been detailed out in the instructions below. Sometimes sourdough starter is used in the dough and other times yeast is used. To keep things as simple as possible, I have used yeast in this dough. But what makes this dough special is that it is folded with a big slab of butter to create thin puffy layers once baked. It's buttery and flaky, but also fluffy and soft and so worth the practice and effort—I promise it gets easier but this recipe gives you all the tips and step-by-step photos to succeed. The key? Don't skimp on the good butter! We're talking minimum 85 percent fat content, ok?

Active Time: 1 hour

Total Time: 4 hours

Yeasted Dough

500 g (4 cups) all-purpose flour

50 g (¼ cup) granulated sugar

15 g (1 tbsp + 1 tsp) instant yeast (2 packets)

250 ml (1 cup + 2 tsp) milk, lukewarm

1 large egg

60 g (¼ cup) butter, softened

1 tsp vanilla extract

Butter Layer

300 g (1⅓ cups) butter, cold (85% fat or more)

Dough

In the bowl of a stand mixer, whisk together the flour, sugar and yeast. Add in the milk, egg, butter and vanilla. Use the dough hook to knead together for 5 minutes on medium-low speed, until the ingredients are just combined. Line a quarter-sized baking sheet with a piece of plastic wrap (it can also be a tray that fits in your refrigerator), place the dough onto the plastic wrap and gently press the dough into a rectangle about the size of the quarter-sized sheet. Lay another piece of plastic wrap on top and place it in the refrigerator for 30 minutes.

Butter Layer

While the dough rests, prepare two sheets of parchment paper that are at least 12 x 12 inches (31 x 31 cm). Draw a rectangle on one sheet of the parchment paper that measures 9 x 9 inches (23 x 23 cm). After the 30 minutes have passed, take the butter out of the refrigerator and cut it into slabs that are about ½ inch (1.3 cm) thick. Flip the paper with the square over so the drawn square is face down. Lay the slabs of butter on the parchment paper inside of the square. It is best if they are all towards the center of the square, not the edges.

Lay the second sheet of parchment paper on top of the butter. Use a rolling pin to pound the butter from the center out towards the edges of the square. This will be loud but you can apologize to any neighbors with the finished pastries.

Once the butter has almost reached the edges, roll the rolling pin over the top with a decent amount of force to get the butter to the edges. If the butter goes over any lines, peel the top layer of parchment away, just at the edge, and use a knife to cut the extra butter away and place it in an area that needs more butter. If needed, you can also use a bench scraper over the top of the parchment, to squeeze the butter that has passed over the line back into the square. Leave the butter wrapped in parchment paper and place it flat in the refrigerator for 10 minutes.

(continued)

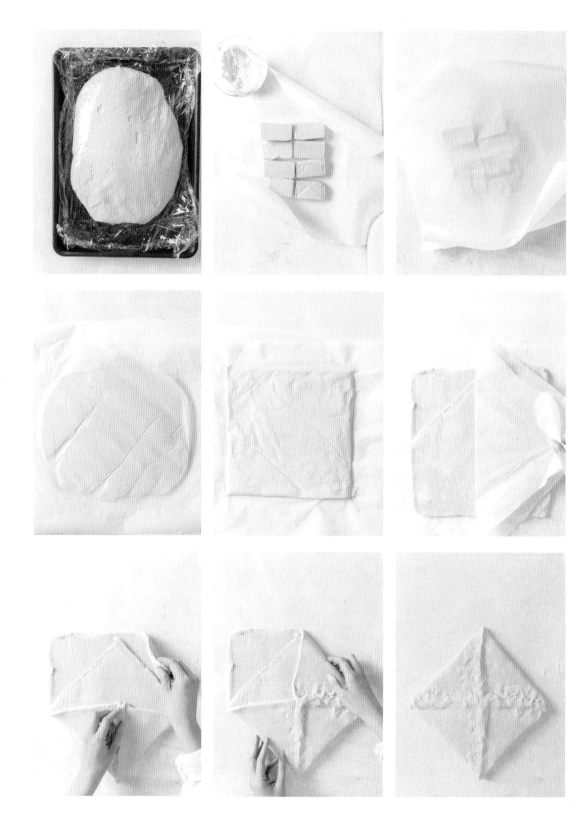

After 10 minutes, take the chilled dough out of the refrigerator but leave the butter inside. Using as little flour as possible, gently roll the dough out into a square that is 13 x 13 inches (33 x 33 cm). It's important that the square is as precise as possible, so use a bench scraper to straighten out edges as needed.

Take the butter out of the refrigerator and peel the parchment paper off of one side of the butter slab. Place the butter diagonally onto the dough so that the corners of the butter hit the middle of each side of the dough and peel away the second piece of parchment. Bring the corners of the dough to the center of the butter slab and seal the edges of the dough together so that all four corners of dough meet in the center of the butter and all edges of dough are sealed. Dust the dough and work surface with flour and use the rolling pin to press the butter and dough together. You want to press hard enough to smush them together, but not so hard that you break the butter. Roll the now sealed butter and dough, following the same direction that you smushed the layers together, into a rectangle that measures 12 x 15 inches (30 x 48 cm). Rotate and flip the dough as necessary. Once rolled out, trim both short ends so that they are neat. Letter fold the dough by folding the dough into thirds. Once folded, the dough should be approximately 5 x 12 inches (13 x 30 cm).

Rewrap the dough in plastic, place it back on the baking sheet, and back into the refrigerator for 40 minutes to chill. Proper chilling time will depend somewhat on the temperature of the room you are working in. When you go to roll the dough out, if the butter seems too hard when you smush it and breaks apart in the dough (you'll see it through the dough), let it warm up gently for a couple more minutes. On the other hand, if the butter is too warm, it will melt into the dough. A good way to check to make sure the butter is the right temperature is when you trim the edges, you should be able to see some amount of layering of butter and dough.

After the chilling time, take the dough back out of the refrigerator. Place it in front of you so that it is taller than wide. Repeat the process of pressing the rolling pin into the dough—this helps the dough and butter become more malleable. Roll the dough out so that the 12-inch (30-cm) edges become 16 inches (40 cm) and the 5-inch (13-cm) edges become 12 inches (30 cm). Trim the short ends to create crisp clean edges. Repeat the letter fold as before, rewrap and place back in the refrigerator for 40 more minutes. Repeat the pressing, rolling, folding and chilling process two more times. After the last chill, it is ready to be used!

Notes

This is probably one of the most difficult recipes in the book because it takes practice, but it is so worth it once you figure it out—just don't expect your first try to be perfect.

The key to this recipe is using a European-style butter with at least 85 percent fat.

DARK CHOCOLATE PASTRY ROLLS |
Schoko Franzbrötchen

Servings: 11–12

Chocolate is not as common in German pastries but let me tell you, these dark chocolate pastry rolls make my chocolate-loving heart so happy. *Franzbrötchen* are a specific type and shape of pastry, most commonly found in northern Germany, especially in Hamburg. Traditionally, they are made with a flaky, buttery dough and layered with cinnamon sugar; however, there are now so many different fillings and toppings available.

This recipe uses the same laminated, yeasted, dough, but it's rolled up with a dark chocolate filling. And then they're topped with a little more chocolate after they come out of the oven that gets all melty and delicious—kind of like a warm chocolate croissant!

Active Time: 45 minutes

Total Time: 6 hours 15 minutes

1 batch of Laminated Dough (page 87)

195 g (7 oz) 60% dark chocolate, roughly chopped, divided

30 g (2 tbsp) butter

70 g (⅓ cup+ 1 tsp) granulated sugar

20 g (3½ tbsp) cocoa powder

40 ml (2 tbsp + 2 tsp) heavy cream

Powdered sugar, for dusting (optional)

Note

These can be made and assembled the night before and then stored in the refrigerator overnight and baked in the morning. Just be sure to give them enough time outside of the refrigerator to come to room temperature and rise.

During the second-to-last chilling of the laminated dough, prepare the chocolate filling. In a large microwave-safe bowl (this can also be done in a sauce pot), add in 80 grams (3 oz) of the roughly chopped chocolate and the butter. Melt in the microwave for 30 seconds and then stir to combine. If necessary, microwave again in 15-second increments until fully melted.

Once melted, whisk in the granulated sugar and cocoa powder, followed by the heavy cream. Set aside to cool. Roughly chop the chocolate for the topping and set it aside in a separate bowl.

Once the laminated dough has chilled fully for the last time, it is time to assemble. Line two baking sheets with parchment paper. Use a rolling pin to roll the completed dough out to 12 x 24 inches (30 x 60 cm). Spread the chocolate filling over the dough, all the way to the edges. Roll the dough up from one long side to the other. With the seam side of the roll down, mark 2-inch (5-cm) cuts onto the roll.

Slice the roll at each mark. Place five to six rolls on each baking sheet with the seam sides down.

Use the handle of a wooden spoon to press down in the center of each roll, parallel to the cut sides of the roll. Be careful not to press through the dough and break it. Then, gently press each one down with the palm of your hand.

Drape the baking sheets with plastic wrap and leave somewhere slightly warm (not hot or the butter will melt) to rise for 1 to 2 hours until they are proofed and jiggly. While they proof, preheat the oven.

Arrange two racks in the oven so they split the oven into thirds. Preheat the oven to 425°F (218°C).

Once proofed for an hour or two and puffy, bake the pastries for 8 minutes. After 8 minutes, swap and rotate the baking sheets 180 degrees. Bake for another 7 to 12 minutes, until they are deep golden brown.

Once baked, take the pastries out of the oven and place the baking sheets on wire racks to cool. While still hot, sprinkle the remaining chopped chocolate along the center pressed line of each pastry. Optionally dust with powdered sugar.

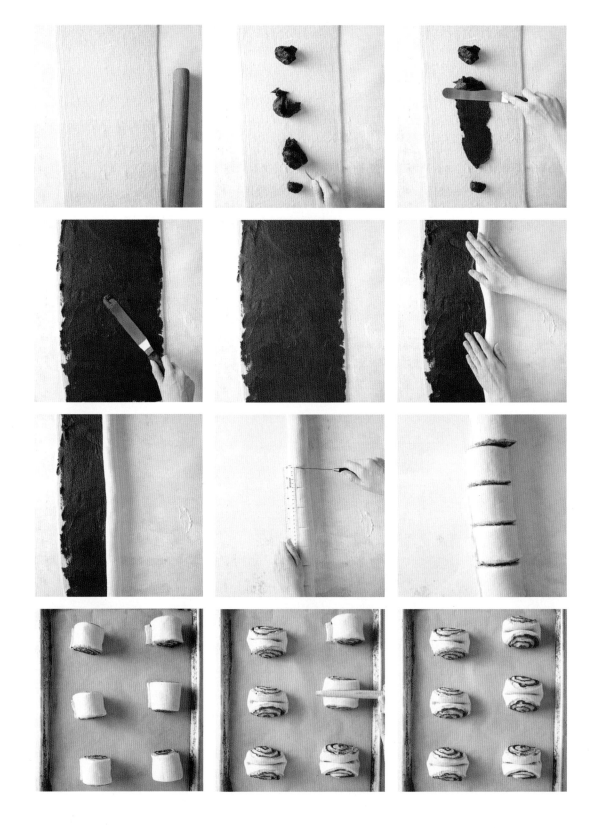

SWEET RAISIN ROLLS |
Rosinenschnecken

Servings: 11–12

If I'm going into a German bakery, there's a 99 percent chance I'm leaving with a schnecke. Directly translated, schnecken are snails, which is incredibly descriptive of the shape, just maybe not the most appealing of names when translated. Made with a yeasted laminated dough and filled with soaked raisins, these *Rosinenschnecken* are a classic at almost every bakery in Germany. Thanks to the *plunderteig*, which is a combo of a yeasted dough and a laminated dough, they're fluffy, flaky and buttery all in one. Plus, the rum-soaked raisin filling and lemon glaze topping make these anything but bland. If you can't stand raisins, swap them for cranberries or chopped dried cherries, but I promise they're yummy with the raisins.

Active Time: 45 minutes

Total Time: 6 hours 15 minutes

---

1 batch of Laminated Dough (page 87)

125 g (¾ cup + 2 tbsp) raisins

30 ml (2 tbsp) rum

110 g (½ cup) marzipan

1 egg white

50 g (3 tbsp + 2 tsp) brown sugar

¼ tsp almond extract

200 g (1⅔ cups) powdered sugar

45 ml (3 tbsp) lemon juice, plus more as needed

Notes

These can be made and assembled the night before and then stored in the refrigerator overnight and baked in the morning. Just be sure to give them enough time outside of the refrigerator to come to room temperature and become puffy.

For an alcohol-free version, soak the raisins in water and a teaspoon of vanilla extract.

During the second to last chilling of the laminated dough, prepare the raisin filling. In a small microwave-safe bowl, combine the raisins and rum. Microwave on high for 30 seconds and set aside to let the raisins absorb the rum and cool down. In the bowl of a stand mixer, add in the marzipan (broken up into small pieces), egg white, brown sugar and almond extract.

Use the paddle attachment to beat the mixture on medium-low speed until smooth. This can take a little while, so don't get discouraged if it doesn't happen immediately. If necessary, turn the speed up to medium. Once smooth, scrape the filling into a bowl and set it aside until the dough is ready.

Once the laminated dough has chilled fully for the last time, it is time to assemble. Line two baking sheets with parchment paper. Roll the dough out to 12 x 24 inches (30 x 60 cm). Spread the marzipan filling over the dough leaving a ¾-inch (2-cm) border on one short side. Sprinkle the rum-soaked raisins over the top of the filling.

Roll the dough up from the short side with no border to the opposite side with the ¾-inch (2-cm) border. With the roll seam side down, mark the roll every inch (2.5 cm). Use a thin, sharp knife to cut the roll into 11 to 12 slices. Clean the knife between slices if it starts to stick and gets hard to cut through. Place six slices on each lined baking sheet, laying the end slices with the pretty cut side up. Tuck about ¾ inch (2 cm) of the end from each roll underneath the roll.

Drape a piece of plastic wrap over each baking sheet. Leave to proof until they are puffy and a little jiggly, about an hour or two. Preheat the oven in the meantime.

Arrange two racks in the oven so they split the oven into thirds and preheat the oven to 425°F (218°C). Once proofed, bake the pastries for 8 minutes. After 8 minutes, swap and rotate the baking sheets 180 degrees. Bake for another 7 to 12 minutes, until they are deep golden brown.

While baking, whisk together the powdered sugar and lemon juice to make the glaze.

Once baked, take the pastries out of the oven and place the baking sheets on wire racks to cool. Brush or drizzle with the lemon glaze until fully coated. Leave to cool until just warm before enjoying.

POPPYSEED SNAILS | Mohnschnecken Servings: 11–12

Named "snails" because of their shape, these poppyseed pastries are hard to beat with the subtle, nutty flavor of poppyseeds—and a touch of lemon, because what are poppyseeds without lemon, especially when they're all wrapped up in flaky, buttery pastry dough? These make the perfect addition to any weekend brunch.

If you're new to the actual flavor of poppyseed and not just a few mixed into a lemon poppyseed muffin, these are another great recipe to get to know what poppyseeds really taste like. They're a little nutty and earthy in flavor and add so much depth to any sweet! If you can, I recommend buying poppyseeds in bulk rather than in spice containers, as it tends to be much more cost-effective.

Active Time: 45 minutes

Total Time: 6 hours 15 minutes

---

1 batch of Laminated Dough (page 87)

150 g (1 cup + 1 tbsp) poppyseeds

75 g (⅓ cup+ 2 tsp) granulated sugar

150 ml (½ cup + 2 tbsp) milk

1 lemon, zested

45 g (3 tbsp) butter

200 g (1⅔ cups) powdered sugar

45 ml (3 tbsp) lemon juice, more as needed

During the second to last chilling of the laminated dough, prepare the poppyseed filling. In a medium-sized sauce pot, add in the poppyseeds, sugar and milk. Stir to combine. Cook over medium heat, stirring frequently for 10 minutes, until the mixture has thickened and most of the milk has evaporated Cooking the poppyseeds first enhances the flavor; if you prefer, you can also grind the poppyseeds in a spice grinder before cooking them.

Once cooked, remove the mixture from the heat and stir in the lemon zest and butter until melted. Transfer to a shallow dish and set it aside to cool to room temperature. This should take 30 minutes if stirred occasionally.

Once the laminated dough has chilled fully for the last time, it is time to assemble. Line two baking sheets with parchment paper. Roll the dough out to 12 x 24 inches (30 x 60 cm). Spread the poppyseed filling over the dough leaving a ¾-inch (2-cm) border on one short side.

Roll the dough up from the short side with no border to the opposite side with the ¾-inch (2-cm) border. With the roll seam side down, mark the roll every inch (2.5 cm). Use a thin, sharp knife to cut the roll into 11 to 12 slices. Place six slices on each lined baking sheet, laying the end slices with the pretty cut side facing up. Tuck about ¾ inch (2 cm) of the end from each roll underneath the roll. Drape a piece of plastic wrap over each baking sheet. Leave them to proof until they are puffy and a little jiggly, about an hour or two. Preheat the oven in the meantime.

Arrange two racks in the oven so they split the oven into thirds and preheat the oven to 425°F (218°C). Once proofed, bake the pastries for 8 minutes. After 8 minutes, swap and rotate the baking sheets 180 degrees. Bake for another 7 to 12 minutes, until they are deep golden brown.

While baking, whisk together the powdered sugar and lemon juice to make the glaze.

Once baked, take the pastries out of the oven and place the baking sheets on wire racks to cool. Brush or drizzle with the lemon glaze until they are fully coated. Leave them to cool until they are just warm.

Note

These can be assembled the night before, stored in the refrigerator overnight and baked in the morning. Just be sure to give them enough time outside of the refrigerator to come to room temperature and become puffy.

HAZELNUT PASTRY TWISTS | Nußschleifen   Servings: 15

Two layers of flaky pastry dough filled with toasted and chopped hazelnuts, brown sugar and marzipan, twisted and baked and then topped with a paper-thin glaze, this is the pastry you never knew you needed. If you don't like the taste of marzipan, don't worry, you won't taste it here—it simply adds moisture and a little nuttiness to the pastries! If you like almond croissants, there's a good chance you'll love these!

If you've ever had *Nußschnecken* in Germany, these twists have a very similar flavor and texture. They just have a fun different shape, because why not? Feel free to swap the hazelnuts for your favorite nut, but hazelnuts are the most traditional and most delicious.

Active Time: 1 hour

Total Time: 6 hours 30 minutes

1 batch of Laminated Dough (page 87)

1 egg white

100 g (⅓ cup + 2 tbsp) marzipan

50 g (3 tbsp + 2 tsp) brown sugar

30 ml (2 tbsp) rum

150 g (1⅓ cups) hazelnuts toasted, peeled and chopped

During the second to last chilling of the laminated dough, prepare the nut filling. In the bowl of a stand mixer, add in the egg white and the marzipan, broken up into small pieces. Use the paddle attachment to cream the egg white and marzipan together on medium-low speed until smooth and fully combined. This can take a little while, but be patient.

Once combined, add in the brown sugar and rum and mix again. Toast and peel the hazelnuts by heating them in a large pan over medium heat until the oils start to appear and they start to brown, stirring often to keep them from burning. Pour the toasted hazelnuts onto a kitchen towel and rub the hazelnuts against each other until the skin comes off. Peel as much of the remaining skin off as possible, but it's ok if some stays. Chop the hazelnuts so that the largest piece is ¼ inch (6 mm) in size. Pour the chopped hazelnuts into the marzipan filling and stir to combine.

Once the laminated dough has chilled fully for the last time, it is time to assemble. Line two baking sheets with parchment paper. Roll the dough out to 12 x 24 inches (30 x 60 cm). Spread the nut filling over one half of the dough lengthwise, leaving a ½-inch (1.3-cm) border on both short sides and the one long side that has the filling. Fold the half of the dough without filling over the other half of the dough. Gently press down to seal everything together. If needed, use a rolling pin to carefully smush it together.

Use a sharp knife to trim off both short sides. Cut the dough into 1½-inch (4-cm) strips. Then, cut a slit down the center of each strip lengthwise but leave a ½ inch (1.3 cm) uncut on both ends so the two sides hold together. Working with one strip at a time, fold the folded edge of dough into the slit and pull it out the other side. Repeat with the opposite end, folding the opposite way so that each strip is twisted twice.

Lay seven to eight of the twists onto the lined baking sheets so that the ends lie flat. Drape a piece of plastic wrap over each baking sheet. Leave them to proof until they are puffy and a little jiggly, about an hour or two. Preheat the oven in the meantime.

(continued)

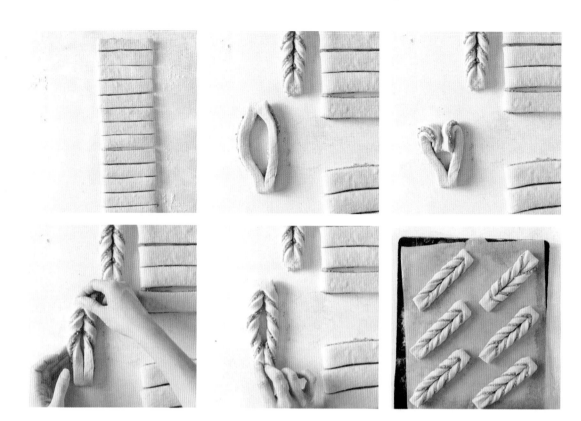

HAZELNUT PASTRY TWISTS | Nußschleifen (continued)

200 g (1⅔ cups) powdered sugar
45 ml (3 tbsp) lemon juice

Note

These can be made and assembled the night before and then stored in the refrigerator overnight and baked in the morning. Just be sure to give them enough time outside of the refrigerator to come to room temperature and become puffy.

Arrange two racks in the oven so they split the oven into thirds and preheat the oven to 425°F (218°C). Once proofed and puffy, bake the pastries for 8 minutes. After 8 minutes, swap and rotate the baking sheets 180 degrees. Bake for another 7 to 12 minutes, until they are deep golden brown.

While baking, whisk together the powdered sugar and lemon juice to make the glaze.

Once baked, take the pastries out of the oven and place the baking sheets on wire racks to cool. Brush or drizzle with the lemon glaze until fully coated. Leave to cool until they are just warm before enjoying.

SWEET PUFF PASTRY HEARTS | Schweinsöhrchen

Servings: 10

Many cultures have some version of *Schweinsöhrchen* (pig ears), such as French *palmiers*. Made from layers of puff pastry folded together with sugar in between, baked until crispy and caramelized, and then dipped in chocolate. Schweinsöhrchen have always been a go-to for my mom, sister and I anywhere we go if we just need a little something sweet.

You will often find them quite large—I'm talking "about the size of your face" large, at bakeries in Germany; however, to achieve that size, the puff pastry needs to be quite long and therefore made from scratch at home. This recipe uses store-bought puff pastry for ease, but you can always make your own at home from scratch, especially if you want to achieve the larger size. If dark chocolate isn't your thing, you can leave them plain or dip them in milk or white chocolate, but dark chocolate will always be my favorite, especially with such a sweet pastry.

Active Time: 30 minutes
Total Time: 1 hour

1 (245-g [8.6 oz]) sheet of puff pastry
100 g (½ cup) granulated sugar, divided

Preheat the oven to 425°F (218°C). Place two racks in the oven so that it divides it into thirds and line two baking sheets with parchment paper.

Defrost the puff pastry. Sprinkle half of the sugar onto your work surface and briefly roll the puff pastry out in one direction so it becomes a little sticky. Cut the sheet of pastry in half lengthwise. Place one sheet, with the sugared side down, on top of the other sheet. Roll the two sheets out together as long as you can, using the remaining sugar as you go to keep the pastry from sticking. You may have to keep pressing the sheets together in the beginning to get them to stick together. Roll until both sheets together are about ¼ inch (6 mm) thick.

As you roll, feel free to flip over the pastry and rotate it as necessary. We want all sides to have sugar stuck to them. Trim the short sides just to even them out. Fold both ends in towards the center leaving about ¼ inch (6 mm) between them. Then, fold it in half so there are four layers on top of each other. Don't worry about pressing it together. Slice the pastry with a sharp knife into slices that are a ½-inch (1.3-cm) wide.

Transfer each folded portion onto the parchment paper. They should be laid in a way that the sliced side is face up and the folded layers are visible. Keep them folded—don't try to spread out the folds and make sure that they are sitting up and they haven't fallen to one side or another. Leave at least 2–3 inches of space between the pastries to allow them room to grow.

Place the baking sheets in the oven for 8 minutes.

After the 8 minutes have passed, take one sheet out of the oven at a time. Working quickly but carefully, use a spatula to flip each one over so the side that was touching the baking sheet is now face up. Then swap the baking sheets and rotate 180 degrees. Flip the pastries on the second baking sheet and bake for another 6 minutes. Once baked and golden brown, take the baking sheets out of the oven and place on wire racks to cool fully.

(continued)

SWEET PUFF PASTRY HEARTS |
Schweinsöhrchen (continued)

120 g (4.2 oz) 60% dark chocolate

In a microwave-safe bowl (big enough to dip the schweinsöhrchen into) or a small sauce pot, microwave the chocolate until it is runny and melted. If melting in the microwave, do so in short bursts of 15 to 30 seconds, stirring in between each burst.

Dip the top tips of the cooled pastries into the melted chocolate, for the most traditional look you can also dip the sides or just drizzle the chocolate on top. Wiggle the pastries back and forth to allow any excess chocolate to drip off, and then place them back on the parchment. Repeat the dipping process for the remaining pastries and leave them to set at room temperature or place them in the refrigerator to speed up the process.

Notes

Be careful when flipping the pastries mid-bake, as they are quite soft and can easily break, so use a large spatula to lift the entire pastry.

If you make your own puff pastry, and want them larger, simply make the sheets bigger and longer so that each folded side will be longer. Don't try to roll the store-bought pastry longer to achieve that length, as it will become too thin and won't puff properly.

SWEET BREAD ROLLS WITH APRICOT JAM | Rohrnudeln

Makes: 9 rolls

Rohrnudeln are basically the definition of simple but delicious. Light and fluffy baked buns filled with apricot jam and topped with a dusting of powdered sugar, these Rohrnudeln are nothing fancy, but they're so good at any time of the day or year. They're really a comfort food that makes your kitchen smell good and your soul feel cozy.

Active Time: 45 minutes

Total Time: 3 hours

335–350 g (2⅔–2¾ cups + 1 tbsp) all-purpose flour, plus more as needed

50 g (¼ cup) granulated sugar

8 g (2 tsp) instant yeast (1 packet)

200 ml (¾ cup + 1 tbsp + 1 tsp) milk, lukewarm

1 large egg, room temperature

50 g (3½ tbsp) butter, softened

1 lemon, zested

180 g (¼ cup + 3 tbsp) apricot jam (or jam of your choice)

50 g (⅓ cup) powdered sugar

Vanille Soße (page 140), for drizzling, optional

Notes

These can be filled with any jam but a thicker, fruitier jam is best to prevent it from running out or absorbing too much into the buns.

Please eat them warm and if you have extra, share with a friend!

In the bowl of a stand mixer, whisk together the flour, sugar and yeast. Pour in the lukewarm milk, egg, butter, and lemon zest. Use the dough hook attachment to knead the dough on medium-low speed until it is smooth and no longer sticking to the sides of the bowl. This should take 15 to 20 minutes, but it can take longer.

Shape the dough into a ball and place in a lightly greased bowl (can be the same mixing bowl). Cover the bowl with a lid or plastic wrap and set it somewhere warm to rest for 1 hour or until it has doubled in size.

Grease a 9 x 9–inch (23 x 23–cm) metal baking pan with softened or melted butter. Once doubled in size, knock the air out of the dough and divide it into nine equal portions by weight.

Working with one portion of dough at a time, pat the dough into a circle that is between 4 inches (10 cm) and 5 inches (13 cm) in diameter. Spoon 20 grams (1 tbsp + 1 tsp) of jam into the center of the circle. Bring the edges of the disk up around the jam filling and pinch to close, being careful not to get jam on the edges because it will prevent the dough from sealing.

Flip the little ball over so that the pinched closed side is down on the counter, use your hand in a claw shape over the ball and roll it in a clockwise direction with a little bit of pressure, keeping it seam side down. This will help seal the ball and reincorporate the dough into the bun. Don't roll too hard or the jam will bust out.

Evenly space the filled rolls with the seam side down in the greased pan. Cover with plastic wrap or a kitchen towel and leave them to proof while the oven heats up. Preheat the oven to 350°F (177°C) and place a rack in the center of the oven. Once the oven is hot and the rolls have grown so they are touching on all four sides, place them in the oven and bake for 15 minutes. After 15 minutes, rotate the pan 180 degrees and bake for another 10 minutes, until they are golden brown.

Once they are baked, take the pan out of the oven and place it on a wire rack to cool for 5 to 10 minutes. Dust the tops with powdered sugar and optionally serve with a drizzle of Vanille Soße (page 140).

PLUM & POPPYSEED DONUTS | Germknödel Krapfen

Inspired by one of my wintertime favorites, classic Austrian *Germknödel*, these krapfen have poppyseeds in the actual donut dough, are filled with plum butter, a.k.a. *powidl*, and are dusted with powdered sugar for the full flavor experience. If Lemon & Raspberry Donuts (page 73) are the perfect spring/summer donut, then these are the perfect fall/winter variation.

This flavor combination is such a classic in Austria and Germany, and if you've never tried it, it's a must. The plum butter doesn't have any actual butter in it—it's more like apple butter—and the light dusting of powdered sugar keeps these from being too sickeningly sweet.

Active Time: 1 hour

Total Time: 2–2 hours 30 minutes

---

500 g (4 cups) all-purpose flour

50 g (¼ cup) granulated sugar

15 g (1 tbsp + 1 tsp) instant yeast (2 packets)

250 ml (1 cup + 2 tsp) milk, lukewarm

1 large egg, room temperature

1 large egg yolk

60 g (¼ cup) butter, softened

75 g (½ cup + 1 tsp) poppyseeds

1 lemon, zested

1 tsp vanilla extract

2 L (67.6 fl oz) vegetable oil

In the bowl of a stand mixer, add in the flour, sugar and yeast. Whisk to combine. Add in the milk, egg, egg yolk, butter, poppyseeds, lemon zest, and vanilla extract. Use the dough hook attachment to knead on medium-low until the dough is smooth and the sides of the bowl are clean, for 15 to 20 minutes.

Shape the dough into a ball and place in a lightly greased bowl (can be the same mixing bowl). Cover the dough with a lid or plastic and place it somewhere warm to rise for 45 minutes.

While the dough rises, pour the oil into a Dutch oven or large, heavy-bottomed pot. Place a thermometer into the oil and heat on medium-low until the oil reaches 350°F (177°C). Place a wire rack onto a baking sheet and lay two layers of paper towels on top of the rack.

Once doubled in size, knock the air out of the dough and divide it into 12 portions. Shape each portion into a ball by first flattening it slightly into a disk and then tucking all the edges of the disk under. Shape your hand into a claw over the ball of dough with the smooth side face up. Roll the ball around in your hand on a clean work surface to create tension on the dough and seal the seam on the bottom of the ball. Place the shaped rolls on a well-floured baking sheet or tray and drape a piece of plastic wrap over the top of the rolls to prevent them from drying out.

Once they have grown to almost twice the size, look a bit puffy, and the oil is hot, it's time to fry.

(continued)

PLUM & POPPYSEED DONUTS |
Germknödel Krapfen (continued)

400 g (1⅔ cups) plum butter

100 g (¾ cup + 1 tbsp)
powdered sugar, for dusting

Note

If you put the krapfen in the oil by
hand, dip one side of the dough in
first and let the other side fall away
from you to prevent the oil from
splashing in your direction.

To fry the donuts, use a metal spatula or spider to lift three of the
donuts from the floured sheet (one at a time) and slowly lower them
into the hot oil. Fry for 1 minute and 30 seconds to 2 minutes on one
side until they are golden brown. Use a metal spider to flip them and
fry again for 2 minutes. Use a spider or slotted spoon to lift them out
of the hot oil and place them on the paper towel–lined cooling rack.
Allow the oil to return to 350°F (177°C) if necessary and then add in
three more donuts.

Once cooled to just warm, poke a hole in the side of each krapfen with
the tip of a paring knife. Fit a piping bag with a metal tip and fill with
the plum butter (a ziplock bag with a hole cut into one of the bottom
corners will work too, just not as well). Place the tip of the bag in the
hole of each donut and squeeze about 2 tablespoons and 2 teaspoons
(40 g) of plum butter into each one. Dust the top of each with powdered
sugar and enjoy fresh!

CHOCOLATE CHERRY TWIST |
Schoko Kirsch Zopf

Servings: 14

Basically every day, I have chocolate and I have bread. Without them, where is the joy? Ok so hear me out: this chocolate cherry twist has it all, plus some cherries to get you that much closer to your five-a-day.

Made with a sweet fluffy, yeasted dough, filled with homemade dark chocolate spread and sprinkled with dried tart cherries, this twist is everything and more. The best part is, it doesn't even need a glaze or a drizzle, although a dusting of powdered sugar never hurts anyone. AND eating it still warm and fresh from the oven is highly encouraged, if not required, for ultimate enjoyment.

Active Time: 45 minutes

Total Time: 3 hours

Dough

250 g (2 cups) all-purpose flour

40 g (2 tbsp + 2 tsp) granulated sugar

8 g (2 tsp) instant yeast (1 packet)

125 ml (½ cup + 1 tsp) milk, lukewarm

40 ml (2 tbsp + 2 tsp) butter, melted

¼ tsp kosher salt

Filling

50 g (1.8 oz) 60% dark chocolate, roughly chopped

50 g (3½ tbsp) butter

40 g (2 tbsp + 2 tsp) granulated sugar

10 g (2 tbsp) cocoa powder, natural or Dutch processed

25 ml (1 tbsp + 2 tsp) heavy cream

70 g (¼ cup + 3 tbsp) dried tart cherries

Dough

In the bowl of a stand mixer, whisk together the flour, sugar and yeast. Pour in the lukewarm milk, butter and salt. Use the dough hook attachment to knead the dough on low speed for 10 minutes, until it is smooth. The dough will be stiff but knead it for the full time.

Shape the dough into a ball and place it in a lightly greased bowl (can be the same mixing bowl). Cover the bowl with a lid or plastic wrap and set it somewhere warm to rest for 1 hour or until it has doubled in size. Meanwhile, make the filling.

Filling

In a medium-sized microwave-safe bowl, add in the chocolate and butter. Microwave for 30 seconds and then stir to combine. If there are still chocolate bits, microwave for another 15 seconds and stir until fully melted.

Pour in the sugar, cocoa powder and heavy cream and stir again. Set this aside and allow it to cool so it's a bit thicker. If it is still too runny when the dough is ready, place it in the freezer for a few minutes and then stir, scraping the sides and bottom of the bowl. Repeat until it has a peanut butter consistency.

Line a baking sheet with parchment paper or a silicone baking mat. Once the dough has doubled in size, knock the air out and roll it out to a rectangle that is 10 x 15 inches (25.5 x 38 cm). Because of how stiff the dough is, you shouldn't need much flour.

Spread the chocolate filling over the dough, leaving a ½-inch (12-mm) border on both short sides and one long side. Sprinkle the dried cherries over the top of the chocolate mixture. Starting at the long edge with no border, roll the dough up tight. Then pinch the seam and both ends shut. Place the roll, seam side down on a cutting board and drape a piece of plastic wrap over the top. Place it in the refrigerator for 1 hour.

(continued)

CHOCOLATE CHERRY TWIST |
Schoko Kirsch Zopf (continued)

50 g (⅓ cup + 1 tbsp) powdered sugar, for dusting

Notes

Wrap leftovers in plastic and freeze in a freezer bag for up to 2 months. When you are ready to enjoy them, defrost them for 1 to 2 hours at room temperature.

If you can't find dried tart cherries, you can also use dried cranberries, dried currants or leave the dried fruit out altogether.

After an hour, preheat the oven to 350°F (177°C) and place a rack in the middle of the oven. Take the roll out of the refrigerator and take off the plastic. Place the roll back on the cutting board and cut in half lengthwise with a thin sharp knife.

Twist both halves together starting in the middle to create an "X" and then twisting until the ends. Be sure the chocolate filling is face up and visible. Pinch the ends of both halves together at each end.

Place the twist on the baking sheet and tuck the pinched ends under the twist. Drape the plastic back over the twist and leave it to proof until it has grown somewhat (it won't double in size) and looks puffy. Once proofed, bake the twist in the hot oven for 15 minutes. Then, rotate the pan 180 degrees and bake for another 10 minutes.

Once baked and golden brown, take the pan out of the oven and place it on a wire rack to cool for 20 to 30 minutes. Once cooled to room temperature, dust the top with powdered sugar and slice the twist into 1-inch (2.5-cm) slices.

MUESLI BREAD | Müsli Brot

I love *müsli*, like I REALLY love it—it's somewhere between oatmeal and granola, and it's the perfect breakfast food. You know what else I love? Freshly baked, crunchy crusted bread with a soft and fluffy inside. And there's really nothing that beats the smell of freshly baked bread in your kitchen, especially when it has dried fruit and oats inside. Well, this Muesli Bread has it all.

When I first started Red Currant Bakery, I baked a lot of bread; I would sell it as a way to pay for my expenses, along with a few other pastries. But the bread was always, without a doubt, everyone's favorite. On days when I would bake a loaf for home, my mom and I would stand around the kitchen island and eat so many slices of the fresh bread, with a layer of her homemade jam on top, because it just made us happy.

P.S. This bread doesn't have to be just sweet. It also makes the perfect grilled cheese or panini bread with any of your favorite toppings!

Active Time: 45 minutes
Total Time: 24 hours

Muesli
100 g (1¾ cups) muesli (a traditional blend with oats, grains, and dried fruit is best)

50 g (⅓ cup) dried fruit, such as dried cranberries or cherries

125 ml (½ cup + 1 tsp) milk

Pre-Dough
100 g (⅔ cup + 1 tbsp) bread flour

8 g (2 tsp) instant yeast (1 packet)

100 ml (⅓ cup + 1 tbsp + 1 tsp) water, room temperature

Main Dough
300 ml (1¼ cups) water, room temperature

50 g (⅓ cup + 1 tbsp) whole wheat flour

400 g (2¾ cups +3 tbsp) bread flour, plus more for rolling

For Dusting
Brown rice flour

Muesli
The night before you plan on baking, combine the muesli, dried fruit and milk in a bowl and stir to combine. Cover the bowl and place it in the refrigerator until the next morning.

Pre-Dough
Just before bed, stir the flour and yeast together in a large glass or plastic bowl (ideally one with a lid). Pour in the water and stir to combine. Lay the lid on top but don't seal it shut.

Main Dough
The next morning, take the muesli out of the refrigerator and set it on the counter. Check on the pre-dough—it should look bubbly and have grown significantly. If so, pour in the 300 milliliters (1¼ cups) of water for the main dough into the bowl with the pre-dough. Use a spoon and stir to combine. If not bubbly, let it sit a little longer somewhere warm. If it looks like it was bubbly but the bubbles have deflated, it is ok to use.

Pour in the whole wheat and bread flour and use your hands to just mix all the ingredients (except the muesli) together, until fully combined. It will be quite sticky. Lay the lid back over the bowl and let it sit for 40 minutes.

Once it has sat for 40 minutes, wet one hand with water. Pretending the bowl has four sides, grab the dough on one side of the bowl, gently pull it out and up and then fold it over the center of the dough. Rotate the bowl 90 degrees clockwise and repeat with the next side of dough. Repeat the turning and folding until all four sides have been folded. Lay the lid back on top and let sit for another 40 minutes.

After the 40 minutes, wet one hand again, then pour about a quarter of the soaked muesli mix onto the top of the dough. Fold one side of the dough over the muesli layer, then sprinkle another quarter of the muesli mix over the dough. Fold another side of the dough. Repeat until all the muesli has been used and all sides have been folded. Lay the lid back on top and let sit for 40 more minutes. Repeat the folding process two more times with 40 minutes of rest in between and after the second time.

(continued)

MUESLI BREAD | Müsli Brot (continued)

Once folded and rested for the last time, prepare a round bread proofing basket or a medium-sized round bowl lined with a towel and dusted with a mixture of 50 percent brown rice flour and 50 percent bread flour—this will help to keep the dough from sticking. Sprinkle the dough and your work surface generously with bread flour. Turn the dough out of the bowl it has been in and onto the floured surface. Pat the dough down to knock the air out.

Using the same folding technique, but now imagining the circle has six sides, fold each side of dough into the center and press down. This dough is sticky, so use more flour as needed.

Flip the dough ball over so that the seam side is down on the work surface. Cup your hands around the back of the ball and gently pull it towards you, turning it slightly as you go. Repeat three to four times or until the dough is sticking to the surface.

Use a bench scraper to help pick up the ball of dough and place it into the bowl or basket that has been dusted with flour. Dust the top and sides of the dough with more flour and cover with a kitchen towel. Immediately turn on the oven.

Place a cast-iron Dutch oven with the lid into the middle of the oven. Then, preheat the oven to 500°F (260°C). This should take about 45 minutes. While the oven is heating up, get out two wire racks and place them close to the oven. Additionally, tear off a sheet of parchment paper, place it near your oven and dust it generously with flour.

Once the oven is hot, uncover the dough and re-dust the top with flour. Tip the dough out of the basket and onto the floured parchment paper. Use thick pot holders, or two together to take the Dutch oven out of the oven and place on one of the wire racks. It will be HOT so be careful. Use the pot holders to lift the lid and place it on the second rack. Use a bench scraper to help lift the dough off of the parchment paper and as carefully as possible, without burning yourself, place it into the Dutch oven.

Immediately, put the lid back on the pot and place it back in the oven. Turn the oven down to 450°F (232°C) and set a timer for 25 minutes. After 25 minutes, take the Dutch oven out of the oven and place it on a wire rack. Take the lid off and place it on the second rack. Return the bottom of the Dutch oven with the bread back into the oven and bake for another 20 minutes, until it is golden brown.

Once baked, take the Dutch oven out of the oven and turn the oven off. Tip onto one of the wire racks and leave it there to cool fully before cutting into it.

Notes

If you forget to start the pre-dough the night before, don't worry, you can also do it when you wake up and just let it sit until it's nice and bubbly. This will just push the baking time back to the evening rather than midday or early afternoon.

If you won't be able to eat the entire loaf in 4 to 5 days, cut it in half and place half in a freezer bag and freeze. To defrost, take it out of the freezer and let it defrost for 4 hours at room temperature in the bag. This will keep the bread fresher than if stored in the fridge where it will dry out.

HAZELNUT CROWN | Nusskranz

In Germany, hazelnuts are one of the most popular nuts, followed closely by almonds. But basically, if you find a sweet nutty treat, odds are pretty high it's going to have hazelnuts in it, which is pretty great if you ask me. Of course, you can swap out the hazelnuts for another nut like almonds, pecans or even walnuts, but I encourage you to really consider it before making such a big (questionable) choice.

Directly translated to nut crown, a *Nusskranz* is a sweet, yeasted dough, filled with a mixture of nuts and sugar, rolled up, cut in half and then twisted into a crown. It's for when you don't feel like making individual rolls, want something nutty and a little sweet and need a show-stopping centerpiece for your breakfast table. There are so many variations of yeasted crowns in Germany, but you really can't go wrong with warm, toasty hazelnuts.

Active Time: 45 minutes

Total Time: 2 hours 30 minutes

Yeasted Dough

325 grams (2½ cups + 1½ tbsp) all-purpose flour

35 g (2 tbsp + 1 tsp) granulated sugar

8 g (2 tsp) instant yeast (1 packet)

150 ml (½ cup + 2 tbsp) milk, lukewarm

1 large egg, room temperature

40 g (3 tbsp) butter, softened

1 lemon, zested

1 tsp vanilla extract

Nut Filling

100 g (⅓ cup + 2 tbsp) marzipan

50 g (3½ tbsp) butter

50 g (3 tbsp + 2 tsp) brown sugar

15 ml (1 tbsp) maple syrup

150 g (1⅓ cups) hazelnuts, toasted, peeled and chopped, divided

Yeasted Dough

In the bowl of a stand mixer, add in the flour, sugar and yeast. Whisk to combine the ingredients. Add in the lukewarm milk, egg, butter, lemon zest and vanilla extract. Use the dough hook attachment to knead on medium-low for 15 minutes, until the dough is smooth and the sides of the bowl are clean.

Shape the dough into a ball and place in a lightly greased bowl. Cover the bowl with a lid or plastic and place somewhere warm to rise for 45 minutes to one hour until it has doubled in size. Preheat the oven to 350°F (177°C) and place a rack in the center of the oven.

Nut Filling

In the bowl of a stand mixer, add in the marzipan (broken up into small pieces), butter, brown sugar and maple syrup. Use the paddle attachment to cream the mixture on medium speed until it is smooth and creamy.

Toast the hazelnuts in a large shallow pan over medium heat until they are slightly browned. Pour the toasted nuts into a kitchen towel and rub them around to peel the hazelnuts (see Note). Then, chop them into ¼-inch (6-mm) chunks. Pour 50 grams (⅓ cup) of the chopped hazelnuts into a separate bowl and set aside.

Once the dough doubled in size, line a baking sheet with parchment paper or a silicone baking mat. Knock the air out of the dough and roll it out to 12 x 18 inches (30 x 45 cm) on a lightly floured work surface.

Spread the marzipan filling over the dough and leave a ½-inch (12-mm) border on both short sides and one long side. Sprinkle the 100 grams (1 cup) of chopped hazelnuts over the filling and press them down gently. Roll the dough up from the long side without a border to the other and squeeze both ends together to seal. Use a long, thin, sharp knife to cut the roll in half lengthwise. Twist the two halves together tightly, with the nut filling face up on both sides. Pinch the ends together.

(continued)

HAZELNUT CROWN | Nusskranz (continued)

Topping

100 g (¾ cup + 1 tbsp)
powdered sugar

2 tbsp (30 ml) lemon juice

75 g (3 tbsp + 2 tsp) apricot jam

Note

Hazelnuts are toasted to remove the skin and enhance the flavor. To do so, put them in a pan over medium heat, stirring often to prevent burning. Once you see the white parts start to brown, pour them onto a kitchen towel. Rub the hazelnuts together with the kitchen towel and the majority of the skin should come off. Peel off as much of the remaining skin by hand as possible, but don't worry if you can't get it all.

Once twisted, bring both ends around and cross them over each other. Tuck the ends under the opposite sides of the twist. Place the crown on the lined baking sheet. Sprinkle the top with the set-aside chopped hazelnuts, gently press into the dough if needed. Drape the crown with a piece of plastic wrap and leave it to proof for 45 minutes (more or less depending on your room temperature) until it has grown about one-and-a-half times its original size.

Bake the crown in the preheated oven for 15 minutes. Then, rotate the pan 180 degrees and bake for another 10 to 15 minutes, until it is golden brown.

Topping

While it bakes, whisk the powdered sugar and lemon juice together to make the lemon glaze.

Once baked, take the baking sheet out of the oven and place it on a wire rack to cool. While still hot, brush the crown with the apricot jam. If necessary, briefly microwave the jam so that it is more easily brushed. Leave it to cool until it is just warm and then drizzle it with the lemon glaze.

PUDDINGS, CREAMS & ICE CREAMS | Puddings, Cremes & Eis

Growing up, one of my favorite treats was to have a bowl of fresh red currants, tossed with sugar and drizzled with a GENEROUS pour of Vanille Soße (page 140)—think of it as melted down vanilla ice cream. The Vanille Soße alone transformed that bowl of delicious berries into one of my all-time favorite summer treats, and that is the power of these recipes.

This chapter is all about the unsung heroes of German desserts. Everything from Vanille Soße (page 140) to *Vanille, Himbeer & Schoko Bayerische Creme* (page 144), not to mention the very necessary ice creams and how to make your own Quark (page 132) from scratch. Puddings, creams and ice creams make up the fillings of cakes, the drizzles on top of your favorite desserts and even a little afternoon snack. Custard is the key to many of these sweets and is the building block of flavor for so many German desserts. This chapter is about the creams that bring it all together.

PUFF PASTRY CREAM SANDWICHES |
Schuhsohlen *(a recipe from my Oma)*

Servings: 9

Schuhsohlen directly translates to "shoe soles" . . . as in the sole of your shoe. I know that might seem a little strange, but in theory, the shape of them is somewhat similar to that of a shoe sole. This is a recipe that I hadn't even heard of until this last year when I was on the phone with my Oma and all of a sudden she tells me about these and how I need to make them. This is a treat that was passed down to her by her mother during the war and was always filled with whatever they had extra of.

Most classically, Schuhsohlen are made with two layers of puff pastry that have been baked with sugar on one side and are then sandwiched with some type of vanilla cream filling. The combination of the crispy and flaky puff pastry works so well with the soft and fluffy vanilla cream. These Schuhsohlen look so impressive but are deceivingly easy to make. This recipe uses homemade vanilla cream but the ultimate lazy hack is to simply use a vanilla pudding mix, but use half as much liquid as the recipe calls for so that it is thick and stiff enough when folded into the whipped cream.

Active Time: 40 minutes

Total Time: 1 hour 40 minutes

Vanilla Cream Filling

14 g (2 tbsp) cornstarch

40 g (2 tbsp + 2 tsp) granulated sugar

150 ml (½ cup + 2 tbsp) milk

1 tsp vanilla extract

100 ml (¼ cup + 1 tbsp + 2 tsp) heavy cream, cold

Puff Pastry

1 (245-g [8.6-oz]) sheet of puff pastry

75 g (¼ cup + 1 tbsp + 2 tsp) granulated sugar, divided

Vanilla Cream Filling

In a small sauce pot, whisk the cornstarch and sugar together. While whisking, slowly pour in the milk. Place the pot over medium heat and cook, whisking continuously until it has thickened and the mixture bubbles at least once, between 5 and 15 minutes. You may need to stop whisking for 5 to 10 seconds to see the bubbles.

Once thickened, remove the pot from the heat and whisk in the vanilla extract. Pour the pudding into a large shallow bowl or dish and lay a piece of plastic wrap over the surface to keep it from forming a skin. Allow the pudding to cool to room temperature—this can take about an hour depending on your home temperature and how shallow the bowl is. Once cooled, you will need to whisk it with an electric mixer to return it to a smooth and soft mixture before using it. The pudding can also be made in advance and stored in the refrigerator until you are ready to use it.

Puff Pastry

Preheat the oven to 400°F (204°C). Place two racks in the oven so that they split the oven into thirds and line two baking sheets with parchment paper. Defrost one sheet of puff pastry, according to package instructions, and roll it out on a lightly floured surface until it's about ⅛ inch (3 mm) thick. Sprinkle one side of the puff pastry with half of the granulated sugar and roll it again so that the sugar is embedded in the dough.

Use a 3-inch (8-cm) circular cutter to cut out as many rounds as possible. Working with one round at a time, sprinkle the same side as before with a ½ teaspoon of sugar. Roll each round out in one direction so that you are left with a very thin oval (you should be able to see light through it). Lay half of the ovals onto each baking sheet, with the sugar side up, and prick the surface four to five times with a fork. Bake the puff pastry ovals for 6 minutes in the preheated oven. Then, swap and rotate the baking sheets 180 degrees, and bake for another 4 minutes so that they bake evenly. Once they are golden brown, remove the baking sheets from the oven and allow the ovals to cool fully, about 10 minutes, before assembling.

(continued)

PUFF PASTRY CREAM SANDWICHES | Schuhsohlen (continued)

Pour the cold heavy cream into the bowl of a stand mixer. Use the whisk attachment to whip the cold heavy cream to stiff peaks on medium-high speed until lines appear and don't disappear when the mixer is turned off. Add half of the whipped cream into the now slightly whipped, cooled pudding and use a rubber spatula to fold the whipped cream in until no streaks remain. Add in the second half of the whipped cream and fold until just combined. If the mixture is too soft, a.k.a. it doesn't hold its shape, place the bowl with the vanilla filling in the refrigerator until it thickens.

Once stiff, place the filling into a piping bag fitted with a round tip. Flip half the ovals over so the non-sugared side is face up, pipe the vanilla cream onto the surface of one of the puff pastry ovals and place a second oval over the top of the filling, gently pressing down. Repeat with the remaining ovals and filling.

Note

These are best eaten right after assembly. If you don't want to eat them all right away, keep the puff pastry ovals in an airtight container at room temperature for up to a couple of days and only assemble as needed.

VANILLA ICE CREAM WITH RASPBERRY SAUCE |
Vanille Eis mit heißen Himbeeren

Makes: ½ gallon or 4 pints (1.9 L)

As I was compiling this book, I asked my mom, who grew up in Germany, what her favorite German desserts were when she was younger, and almost immediately she mentioned *Vanille Eis mit heißen Himbeeren*. She used to have it all the time as a kid and while it's simple, it's too delicious not to have in here.

I love to make Vanilla Bean Ice Cream from scratch, but if you're in a time crunch, you can always use your favorite store-bought or local ice cream shop! The warm raspberry sauce is so simple that you can't even call it a compote. It's simply cooked down frozen raspberries with a few fresh raspberries added into the mix at the end for some texture and brightness. Think of this as a slightly grown-up, simple and elegant ice cream sundae.

Active Time: 45 minutes

Total Time: 24 hours

Ice Cream

450 ml (1¾ cups + 2 tbsp) milk

450 ml (1¾ cups + 2 tbsp) heavy cream

1 vanilla bean

200 g (1 cup) granulated sugar

6 egg yolks

Ice Cream

In a medium-sized sauce pot, pour in the milk and heavy cream. Cut the vanilla bean in half lengthwise. Use the back of a knife to scrape out the seeds into the milk mixture along with the empty vanilla bean pod. Heat the mixture over medium heat, stirring frequently until it is steaming. Remove it from heat, stir a few more times, cover it with a lid, and leave it to steep for 1 to 2 hours. If the pot is still very hot when you take it off the heat, stir it every 5 minutes for the first 15 minutes to keep it from burning the bottom of the pot. Once steeped, remove the lid and scoop out the vanilla bean pod, leaving the seeds.

Heat the milk mixture back over medium heat, stirring frequently until it just begins to bubble. While the milk is heating, add in the sugar and egg yolks to a medium-sized mixing bowl, and whisk to combine. Place the bowl with the egg yolks on a damp rag to prevent it from spinning.

Once the milk mixture is hot, take the pot off the heat and place it next to the bowl with the egg yolks and sugar. While whisking the egg yolks, use a ladle to pour about half of the vanilla liquid into the egg yolk mixture. This is called tempering the eggs and will prevent them from curdling—just don't stop whisking. Then, swap and slowly pour the tempered eggs into the milk in the pot, whisking continuously. Return the pot to medium-low heat and use a rubber spatula to gently stir the custard mixture. Stir in a figure eight pattern and then around the edge of the pot; this will allow the custard to cook evenly.

Continue stirring and cooking until the mixture thickens and the bubbles on the surface have completely disappeared. This can take anywhere from 10 to 20 minutes (or longer, depending on your stove and pot). Once cooked, pour the custard through a fine mesh sieve into a heat-safe bowl. Allow the custard to come to room temperature, whisking every 10 to 15 minutes for about 1 hour. Place a piece of plastic wrap onto the surface of the custard and then place it in the refrigerator to chill overnight. If you're in a hurry, you can place the plastic on the surface immediately, let it come to room temperature, and then place it in the fridge to chill.

(continued)

VANILLA ICE CREAM WITH RASPBERRY SAUCE |
Vanille Eis mit heißen Himbeeren (continued)

Topping

850 g (6 cups + 1 tbsp) frozen raspberries

450 g (3⅔ cups) fresh raspberries

Set up your ice cream maker per the instructions. Once running, slowly stream in the vanilla custard. Churn until it looks like soft serve. Once churned, pour the mixture into the storage container of your choice (I like to line a loaf pan with parchment paper). Then place in the freezer to set for at least 6 hours.

Topping

In a medium sauce pot, add in the frozen raspberries. Cook them over medium-low, stirring occasionally until the mixture just begins to simmer and some of the raspberries have broken apart. Once the mixture is gently bubbling, turn the heat off and quickly stir in the fresh raspberries. Pour approximately 80 grams (⅔ cup) of the warm raspberries over each serving of vanilla ice cream.

Notes

To save time, you can always use store-bought vanilla ice cream or pair the raspberry mixture with any other ice cream of your choice!

Heißen himbeeren can also be added to basically anything your heart desires so it never hurts to have some raspberries on hand.

VANILLA SEMOLINA PUDDING | Grießpudding

Servings: 4–6

Growing up, my mom made us *Grießbrei* for breakfast on cold mornings, which we then proceeded to top with copious amounts of dark chocolate sprinkles, and we thought it was the best thing. Grießbrei is *greiß* cooked with milk or water into a thick porridge, which is really the foundation for this pudding recipe. I love this variation because it's a little sweeter and has a bit more flavor, but still comes together in no time and immediately reminds me of the cold winter mornings when she would make us Grießbrei.

Grießpudding is sweet and creamy, but it's also a little hearty. Grieß is a grain in Germany that comes in both a soft and hard variety. I find that the two best substitutes are Cream of Wheat® and semolina flour. For this pudding, I have used semolina flour which has a bit more texture, but you could also use Cream of Wheat (just don't use the instant version) instead! This sweet is a cross between a porridge and a pudding and makes the perfect afternoon snack, or top it with warm Raspberry Sauce (page 128) for an after-dinner dessert.

Active Time: 20 minutes

Total Time: 30 minutes– 3 hours

Pudding

7 g (1 tbsp) cornstarch

55 g (¼ cup + 1 tsp) granulated sugar

450 ml (1¾ cups + 2 tbsp) milk

¼ teaspoon kosher salt

35 g (3 tbsp) semolina

100 ml (¼ cup + 1 tbsp + 2 tsp) heavy cream

1 tsp vanilla extract

Topping Ideas

Heißen himbeeren from Vanille Eis recipe (page 127)

Cinnamon sugar

Chocolate sprinkles

Fresh fruit

In a medium-sized sauce pot, whisk together the cornstarch and sugar. Slowly whisk in the milk and sprinkle in the salt. Place the pot over medium heat and bring it to a simmer, whisking constantly. Pour in the semolina and cook until it has thickened. If the milk was bubbling, this will happen quickly, within 5 minutes. If it doesn't happen that quickly, don't worry—your milk may not have been quite hot enough. Simply cook for another 5 minutes and it should thicken. It will be quite thick to the point where it is almost difficult to stir, so swap to a wooden spoon or rubber spatula when needed.

Remove the pot from the heat and stir in the heavy cream and vanilla extract. The pudding can be served as-is or portioned into individual bowls and placed in the refrigerator for at least 2 hours, once it has cooled to room temperature, to firm up more like a traditional pudding. Leave it plain or give it a little something with your favorite topping!

Note

This mixture will get quite thick when it cooks, so be sure you are holding on to the pot while stirring once the semolina has been poured in.

QUARK

Quark is a foundational ingredient in German life and baking. It's similar to Greek yogurt, but less tart and more stable when baking. Basically, it's just great. However, it can be very hard to find in the US and countries outside of Europe. When I finally perfected this recipe, I was so excited because it opened up the possibility for so many more of my favorite German recipes including *Mohn Käsekuchen* (page 59), *Sahnetorte* (page 57), and *Quarktaschen* (page 83).

Don't be intimidated by making your own quark—it can take a little getting used to, depending on your stove and the pot you are using, but it is so worth it. I now make a batch of quark every Sunday to have for the week for recipes and just for snacking. This recipe is not only easy, but also inexpensive!

Active Time: 1 hour

Total Time: 24 hours

---

1 L (33.8 fl oz) whole-milk buttermilk (fat-free will also work for most recipes as long as not otherwise specified)

Notes

This quark can be stored in an airtight container in the refrigerator for at least a week.

When heating the buttermilk, low and slow is important. If you heat it too quickly, it will cause the curds to dry out into a crumbly consistency rather than a creamy one.

It is important to use a cheesecloth to strain the quark in order to retain the curds (that are somewhat soft) while straining out the whey.

Pour the buttermilk into a large lidded pot. Cover it with the lid and cook over low heat (until you know your stove, start with the lowest temperature setting). Leave it to sit to heat gently for 20–30 minutes. If it looks like nothing has happened, turn the heat up slightly, but you don't want the buttermilk to bubble at all. You will know the buttermilk is done when you lift the lid, tilt the pot slightly and the buttermilk has separated into a thick white round surrounded by clear liquid. If the white isn't holding together, cook it longer. If it looks like it's about to start bubbling, remove it from the heat immediately. The thick white portion should look somewhat like cottage cheese (lumpy but held together with milkier portions—it'll look a little weird until the very last step so don't get discouraged here). Once it is finished cooking, remove it from heat and leave it to cool, with the lid on, at room temperature for 2 hours.

Place a large fine mesh sieve over a medium-sized bowl and line the sieve with a cheesecloth. Use a slotted spoon to scoop out the white portion and pour it into the lined sieve. Place the bowl with the quark in the sieve in the refrigerator overnight. The clear liquid that is left in the pot won't be needed for the recipe so you can toss it or use it in things like smoothies!

The next day, place the blender jug on your scale and dump the strained quark in. It should be about 600 grams (21.2 oz). If it weighs much more, you will know for next time to cook it a little longer. If it is less than 500 grams (17.6 ounces), it is slightly overcooked—neither is the end of the world, and as long as it isn't more than 650 grams (22.9 oz) or less than 450 grams (15.9 oz), it will still work in recipes. If it is more, enjoy it for breakfast or as a snack but it might not work as well in a recipe. If it it less, pour the excess clear liquid that had strained into the bowl into the blender until it totals 650 grams (22.9 oz) with the strained quark. If you are using low-fat buttermilk, it will have a tendency to produce less. Blend starting on low speed and slowly increasing until smooth. Use a spatula to scrape down the sides as necessary. Once blended and smooth, pour the quark into a lidded container and put it in the refrigerator until you are ready to use it.

BAKED CREAM OF WHEAT SOUFFLÉ | Grießauflauf

Servings: 4–6

Grießauflauf is a light and fluffy cloud-like bake, that will melt in your mouth (if you don't burn it first from lack of patience). Just a little sweet, it should be served hot, straight from the oven with a dusting of powdered sugar and a drizzle of Vanille Soße (page 140) on top.

It's made with Cream of Wheat rather than semolina because I find it keeps the batter a little softer and helps it rise more when baking. Think of this as the perfect breakfast bake, and while it's best fresh from the oven, it's still delicious the next day reheated in the microwave.

Active Time: 20 minutes

Total Time: 1 hour 30 minutes

Batter

750 ml (3 cups + 2 tbsp) milk, divided

75 g (¼ cup + 1 tbsp) granulated sugar

25 g (1 tbsp + 2 tsp) butter

200 g (1 cup + 2 tbsp) Cream of Wheat

1 tsp vanilla extract

4 eggs, separated

Add-Ins

165 g (1 cup + 3 tbsp) frozen raspberries

Topping

30 g (¼ cup) powdered sugar, for dusting

1 recipe Vanille Soße (page 140)

Notes

This will always taste best fresh, but it stores well for 2 to 3 days in the refrigerator and can be reheated in the microwave in individual portions.

You can also leave out the raspberries if you prefer or add in a different berry.

Preheat the oven to 350°F (177° C) and place a rack in the center of the oven. In a medium-sized sauce pot, add in 500 milliliters (2 cups + 1½ tbsp) of milk, the granulated sugar and butter. Heat over medium heat, whisking frequently, until the mixture is bubbling. Keep whisking and pour in the Cream of Wheat and continue to stir until it is thick, for 5 to 10 minutes. Swap to a rubber spatula and cook until the mixture peels away from the bottom of the pot while stirring. Once it is thick, remove it from the heat and pour in the remaining 250 milliliters (1 cup + 2 tsp) of milk and the vanilla extract and stir to combine. Allow the mixture to cool until it is just warm to the touch.

Separate the eggs and place the egg whites in the bowl of a stand mixer and the egg yolks in a separate medium-sized bowl. Whisk the egg whites with the whisk attachment. Start on medium-high speed until they become frothy and then increase the speed to high until stiff peaks form. Depending on the temperature of your egg whites, this will take 3 to 7 minutes. Whisk the egg yolks together with a fork until they are smooth and cohesive. Add the Cream of Wheat mixture into the egg yolks in three additions, stirring between each addition to combine. Then, use a wide rubber spatula to fold half of the whipped egg whites into the Cream of Wheat mixture. Be careful not to knock the air out of the egg whites. To prevent this, use a folding motion, scooping the batter from underneath the egg whites and folding it on top of them. Then, fold in the second half of the egg whites. Lastly, carefully fold in the raspberries.

Grease a 9 x 7–inch (23 x 18–cm) glass baking dish (at least 2½ inches, [6 cm] deep) with butter or a baking spray. Pour the batter into the dish and immediately place it in the preheated oven for 30 minutes. After 30 minutes, rotate the dish 180 degrees and bake for another 10 to 15 minutes, until it is golden brown.

Once baked, remove the dish from the oven and place it on a wire rack to cool for 5 to 10 minutes. Dust with powdered sugar and pour some of the Vanille Soße (page 140) on top of the whole bake. Scoop out the portions to serve and top with a little more of the vanilla sauce.

LEIBNIZ PUDDING SANDWICHES |
Leibniz Pudding Schnitte

It's like an ice cream sandwich but a pudding sandwich, made with the best store-bought cookies and filled with a rich and creamy custard pudding. Eat them like an ice cream sandwich or serve them as pieces of cake and eat them with a fork—either way, they're simple and yummy.

These are so easy and fun to make, plus they're a crowd-pleaser for all ages. You can use any butter- or wafer-style cookie, but dark chocolate Leibniz cookies balance out the sweetness of the pudding perfectly.

Active Time: 30 minutes

Total Time: 24 hours

65 g (½ cup) cornstarch

160 g (¾ cup + 2 tsp) granulated sugar

700 ml (2¾ cups + 2 tbsp + 2 tsp) milk

200 ml (½ cup + ⅓ cup) heavy cream

4 egg yolks

40 g (3 tbsp) butter

10 ml (2 tsp) vanilla extract

24 dark chocolate Leibniz cookies (most other butter cookies will work too)

Notes

If you can't find or don't want to use dark chocolate Leibniz, you can use any other store-bought or home-made butter cookies.

If your cookies don't have chocolate, you can pour a layer of melted choco-late on top of the top layer of cookies after it is set.

In a medium-sized sauce pot, whisk together the cornstarch and sugar. While whisking, slowly pour in the milk and then the heavy cream. Then, add in the egg yolks and whisk again. Place the pot over medium heat and whisk constantly for 10 minutes, until the mixture thickens and lines from the whisk are visible for at least 1 second. Once it starts to bubble, remove it from the heat and do a quick taste test to see if there is any graininess or chalkiness from the cornstarch. If so, put it back over medium-low or low heat and stir constantly with a rubber spatula for a few more minutes.

Once cooked, remove the mixture from the heat and whisk in the butter and vanilla extract until the butter has melted. Pour the pudding into a large shallow dish and allow it to come to room temperature; this will take 1 to 2 hours depending on your room temperature and dish. You either need to stir it every 10 minutes to prevent a skin from forming (this will help it cool quicker) or lay a sheet of plastic wrap onto the surface (this is simpler but can take a little longer) while it cools. Don't put the pudding in the fridge, or it will become too stiff.

Once the pudding has cooled, it's time to assemble. Line the bottom and all sides of a 9 x 9–inch (22 x 22–cm) pan with plastic wrap. Lay the dark chocolate Leibniz with the chocolate side down in an even layer on the bottom of the pan. It's best if you can have them all with sides touching, centered in the pan. All cookies should be going in the same direction; because of their rectangular shape, you should be able to fit 3 across and 4 up and down. Mark one side of the pan with a sticker or some other indicator to let you know which direction the cookies are going. This is important because the top layer needs to be the exact same. Pour the cooled vanilla pudding gently over the top, trying not to shift the cookies. Use a rubber spatula to gently spread the pudding out into an even layer. Place the remaining 12 cookies with the bare cookie side down onto the pudding in the same arrangement you did on the bottom. Place the whole pan in the refrig-erator for at least 12 hours or up to overnight.

The next day, use the plastic wrap to lift the pudding sandwiches out of the pan. Use a long thin sharp knife to trim away the edges of excess pudding, cleaning the knife between each cut.

Then, slice between each cookie to make the cookie pudding sandwiches. These are a little messy to eat but so much fun.

KINDER CHOCOLATE ICE CREAM |
Kinder Eis

Makes: ½ gallon (1.9 L)

This idea came to me after my last trip to Germany. We were walking around one evening after dinner and my mom and I stopped for some ice cream at this shop that had some of the most creative and innovative flavors I had ever seen. One of them was made with one of my favorite chocolate candies, and seeing how creative other people are with their food always inspires me.

The idea to put Kinder chocolates in ice cream seemed so obvious afterwards—simple, rich and creamy vanilla ice cream, infused with melted *Kinder Schokolade* and folded with chopped chunks of more Kinder chocolates. I'm pretty sure this ice cream is every kid's fantasy. It's definitely mine, so I had to bring it to life with this recipe.

Active Time: 30 minutes
Total Time: 24 hours

24 Kinder Riegel®

450 ml (1¾ cups + 2 tbsp) milk

450 ml (1¾ cups + 2 tbsp) heavy cream

200 g (1 cup) granulated sugar

6 egg yolks

10 ml (2 tsp) vanilla extract

Note

The Kinder chocolates that get melted into the custard need to be the Kinder Riegels that have no wafer or hazelnut in them because they melt best. However, for the chocolates that get layered in after the ice cream has been churned, you can choose any of your favorite Kinder chocolates or a mix of multiple!

Finely chop 12 of the Kinder Riegel, place them in a large heat-safe bowl, and place a fine mesh sieve on top. In a medium-sized sauce pot, pour in the milk and heavy cream.

Heat the milk mixture over medium heat, stirring frequently until it just begins to bubble. While the milk is heating, add the sugar and egg yolks to a medium-sized mixing bowl, and whisk to combine. Place the bowl with the egg yolks on a damp rag to prevent it from spinning.

Once the milk mixture is hot and steaming, take the pot off the heat. While whisking the egg yolks, use a ladle to pour about half of the liquid into the egg yolk mixture. This is called tempering the eggs and will prevent them from curdling—just don't stop whisking. Then, swap and slowly pour the tempered eggs into the milk in the pot, while whisking the milk continuously. Return the pot to medium-low heat and use a rubber spatula to gently stir the custard mixture. It's best to stir the custard in a figure eight pattern and then around the pot, alternating between the two to distribute the heat evenly.

Continue stirring and cooking for 10 to 20 minutes, until the mixture thickens and the little bubbles on the surface have completely disappeared. Once cooked, pour the custard through the sieve into the bowl with the chopped-up Kinder Riegel. Add in the vanilla extract and stir to combine. Allow the custard to come to room temperature, whisking every 10 to 15 minutes, for 1 hour. Place a piece of plastic wrap onto the surface of the custard and then place it in the refrigerator to chill overnight.

Set up your ice cream maker per the instructions. Once running, slowly stream in the Kinder *schoko* custard. Churn until it looks like soft serve. Once churned, pour one-third of the mixture into the storage container of your choice (I like to line a loaf pan with parchment paper), break up four of the Kinder Riegel and crumble them on top of the ice cream. Pour another third of the ice cream on top and crumble four more Kinder Riegel on top. Repeat this process one more time with the remaining ice cream and Kinder Riegel. Then, place the ice cream in the freezer to set for at least 6 hours.

VANILLA CUSTARD SAUCE |
Vanille Soße

I have a confession to make: any time I make Vanille Soße and have to pour it into a container, I leave a little extra in the pot that I get to scoop out with the rubber spatula because I love it so much.

Vanille Soße is a vanilla custard sauce that is kind of magical because it basically tastes AMAZING on everything, from a variety of German sweets to a bowl of fresh fruit (especially red currants). Essentially any time you think of putting vanilla ice cream or cream on top of a dessert, consider using Vanille Soße instead. The vanilla bean adds to the flavor and of course looks beautiful, but you can always add 10 milliliters (2 tsp) of vanilla extract if you can't get your hands on a vanilla bean.

Active Time: 15 minutes
Total Time: 2 hours

1 vanilla bean
300 ml (1¼ cups) milk
75 g (⅓ cup + 2 tsp) granulated sugar
3 egg yolks

Split a vanilla bean in half and scrape out the inside into a medium-sized sauce pot. Add in the milk and sugar and place the pot over medium heat, stirring frequently until it starts to steam and the sugar is fully dissolved.

In the meantime, place the egg yolks in a medium-sized bowl and whisk until smooth. Place the bowl on a damp rag or kitchen towel to prevent it from slipping.

Once the milk is heated, turn the heat off and slowly whisk 120 milliliters (½ cup) of the milk mixture into the egg yolks to temper them. While stirring the remaining milk mixture continuously, pour the egg mixture back into the sauce pot and raise the heat to medium-low, swap to a rubber spatula and stir frequently. Cook for 10 to 15 minutes, until the sauce thickens slightly and coats a wooden spoon.

Turn off the heat, pour the mixture through a fine mesh sieve into a container and cover with plastic wrap on the surface to prevent it from forming a skin. Cool it to room temperature for an hour before refrigerating it until needed.

Note

This can be stored in the refrigerator for 4 to 5 days.

RASPBERRY ICE CREAM |
Himbeer Eis

Makes: ½ gallon or 4 pints (1.9 L)

Coming in close behind red currants, raspberries are without a doubt my second favorite fruit. If I could, I would eat boxes and boxes of them all year long, and if I'm not going for chocolate, chances are pretty high that I'm going for raspberry when it comes to ice cream. This raspberry ice cream is full of raspberry flavor but still soft and creamy and makes the perfect filling in the Raspberry Ice Cream Chocolate Cake (page 39).

Active Time: 30 minutes
Total Time: 24 hours

---

500 g (3½ cups + 1 tbsp) frozen raspberries

250 ml (1 cup + 2 tsp) milk

400 ml (1⅔ cups) heavy cream

6 egg yolks

200 g (1 cup) granulated sugar

1 tsp vanilla extract

Note

This recipe could also be made with other berries, but I recommend choosing ones that aren't too watery. Fruit such as cherries, blueberries or red currants would be great in this ice cream.

Defrost the raspberries and smush them with a fork or potato masher into a large bowl. Place a fine mesh sieve over the top and set them aside.

In a medium-sized sauce pot, add in the milk and heavy cream. In a separate medium-sized mixing bowl, add in the egg yolks.

Heat the milk mixture over medium heat, stirring frequently until it just begins to bubble. While the milk is heating, add the sugar to the bowl with the egg yolks and whisk to combine. Place the bowl with the egg yolks on a damp rag to prevent it from spinning.

Once the milk mixture is hot, take the pot off the heat. While whisking the egg yolks, use a ladle to pour about half of the liquid into the egg yolk mixture. This is called tempering the eggs and will prevent them from curdling—just don't stop whisking. Then, swap and slowly pour the tempered eggs into the milk in the pot, whisking the milk continuously. Return the pot to medium-low heat and use a rubber spatula to gently stir the custard mixture. Continue stirring and cooking until the mixture thickens and the little bubbles on the surface have completely disappeared. This can take anywhere from 10 to 20 minutes (or longer depending on your stove and pot).

Once cooked, pour the custard through the fine mesh sieve into the bowl with the raspberries. Add in the vanilla extract and stir to combine. Allow the custard to come to room temperature, whisking every 10 to 15 minutes for about an hour. Place a piece of plastic wrap onto the surface of the custard and then place it in the refrigerator to chill overnight.

The next day, set up your ice cream maker per the instructions. Once running, slowly stream in the raspberry custard. Churn until it looks like soft serve ice cream. Once churned, pour the mixture into the storage container of your choice (I like to line a loaf pan with parchment paper). Then place the ice cream in the freezer to set for at least 6 hours.

VANILLA, RASPBERRY & CHOCOLATE BAVARIAN CREAM | Vanille, Himbeer & Schoko Bayerische Creme

Servings: 8

Bavarian Cream has always been one of my mom's and my favorite desserts; it's an "eat-it-straight-from-the-bowl-with-two-spoons" kind of love, so it obviously needed to be in this book. Raspberry, chocolate and vanilla are without a doubt three of the best flavors, and eating them all together in Bavarian cream form is even better. Bavarian cream is folded with heavy cream rather than egg whites, which gives it a richer and creamier feel than mousse. It's also set with gelatin rather than cooked with cornstarch, which helps give it a light and airy texture as opposed to a traditional pudding. Serve this in clear glasses at your next dinner party for a guaranteed show-stopper.

Active Time: 45 minutes

Total Time: 12 hours

75 g (2.6 oz) 60% dark chocolate, finely chopped

150 g (1 cup + 1 tbsp) frozen raspberries, defrosted

260 ml (1 cup + 1 tbsp + 1 tsp) milk, cold, divided

7–8 g (2 tsp) gelatin (1 packet)

550 ml (2¼ cups + 2 tsp) heavy whipping cream, divided

5 egg yolks

50 g (¼ cup) granulated sugar

10 ml (2 tsp) vanilla extract

Note

The gelatin can be left out for a less traditional Bavarian cream; if you are in a hurry and don't have time to let it sit, it can be made without gelatin and served almost immediately. But unless you are strongly opposed, I highly recommend giving gelatin a chance.

In a medium-sized bowl, melt the finely chopped chocolate and set aside.

Blend the defrosted raspberries in a blender, pour through a sieve into a medium-sized bowl, and set aside.

Place 56 milliliters (¼ cup) of milk in a medium-sized bowl and sprinkle the top with the powdered gelatin and stir together. Place a fine mesh sieve on top and set aside while preparing the custard. Pour 150 milliliters (½ cup and 2 tbsp) of the cream and the remaining 204 milliliters (¾ cup + 1⅓ tbsp) of milk into a medium-sized sauce pot and cook on the stove over medium heat until it starts to simmer, stirring frequently. While the cream and milk heat up, whisk the egg yolks and sugar together in a medium-sized bowl until they are light and frothy. Place the bowl on a damp cloth to prevent it from slipping. Once the cream mixture is heated through and steaming, remove it from the heat.

While whisking the egg yolk mixture constantly, use a ladle to slowly pour about 120 milliliters (½ cup) of the hot cream mixture into the egg yolks and sugar. This is called tempering the eggs. Now, while whisking the remaining cream in the sauce pot, slowly pour the now tempered egg mixture back in.

Return the pot to medium heat and stir constantly with a rubber spatula. Continue heating and stirring for 10 to 15 minutes, until the mixture has thickened slightly—thick enough to coat the back of a wooden spoon. Once thickened, remove it from the heat immediately and pour it through the sieve over the bloomed gelatin. Remove the sieve and add in the vanilla extract and then then whisk the gelatin into the custard.

Immediately pour one-third of the custard into the bowl with finely chopped chocolate. Whisk to combine. Pour another third of the custard into the raspberry puree. Whisk the vanilla, raspberry and chocolate creams frequently for 20 minutes, until almost cooled to room temperature.

(continued)

VANILLA, RASPBERRY & CHOCOLATE BAVARIAN CREAM | Vanille, Himbeer & Schoko Bayerische Creme (continued)

Once the chocolate mixture has cooled to room temperature, pour the remaining 400 milliliters (1⅓ cups) of cold heavy whipping cream into the bowl of a stand mixer. Use the whisk attachment to whip the cream to medium stiff peaks on medium-high speed. It should hold lines for 5 to 10 seconds. Fold one-third of the cream into the chocolate mixture. Divide the chocolate mixture into the eight glasses with a small ladle. Place the glasses in the refrigerator while preparing the raspberry layer. Fold another third of the whipped cream into the raspberry puree. Check the top of the chocolate layer to see if it has just barely started to firm up. If so, gently ladle the raspberry layer on top of the chocolate layer, being careful not to let it break the surface of the chocolate layer. If necessary, leave the glasses with the chocolate layer in the refrigerator for a few more minutes.

Place the glasses back in the refrigerator and fold the remaining cream into the vanilla layer.

Once the raspberry layer has just barely thickened, take the glasses out of the refrigerator and add the vanilla layer on top. These can be served immediately but are traditionally left to set overnight. Serve the next day as is or topped with fresh whipped cream, raspberries, or chocolate shavings.

LEMON ICE CREAM |
Zitronen Eis

Makes: ½ gallon or 4 pints (1.9 L)

One of my favorite parts about visiting Germany in the summer is the ice cream, specifically the Lemon Ice Cream. If there was ever an afternoon where we didn't stop for kaffee und kuchen, my sister and I would always find the closest ice cream shop and get scoops of *Zitronen Eis*. It's light and smooth without being icy like sorbet or overly creamy like vanilla ice cream. This lemon ice cream is perfect on a waffle cone on a hot summer day or in your favorite ice cream bowl!

This recipe uses less heavy cream than other ice creams to really allow the tart lemon to shine through! And if you really want to dress this one up, cut fresh lemons in half, trim off ½ inch (1.3 cm) from each end and scoop out the insides. Fill each lemon cup with a scoop of ice cream and freeze for at least an hour or two on a tray before serving!

Active Time: 30 minutes

Total Time: 24 hours

750 ml (3 cups + 2 tbsp) milk

250 ml (1 cup + 2 tsp) heavy cream

200 g (1 cup) granulated sugar, divided

3 egg yolks

1 lemon, zested

125 ml (½ cup + 1 tsp) lemon juice

Note

If you don't have time to whisk the custard as it cools, simply put a piece of plastic wrap on the surface while it cools down to room temperature and then place it in the refrigerator once it has reached room temperature.

In a medium-sized sauce pot, pour in the milk, heavy cream and 100 grams (½ cup) of sugar. In a separate medium-sized mixing bowl, add in the egg yolks. Heat the milk mixture over medium heat, stirring frequently until it just begins to bubble. While the milk is heating, add the remaining 100 grams (½ cup) of sugar to the egg yolks and whisk to combine. Place the bowl with the egg yolks on a damp rag to prevent it from spinning.

Once the milk mixture is hot, remove the pot from the heat and use a ladle to pour about half of the liquid into the egg yolk mixture while whisking the egg yolks constantly. This is called tempering the eggs and will prevent them from curdling—just don't stop whisking. Then, swap and slowly pour the tempered egg mixture back into the pot while whisking the remaining milk mixture. Return the pot to medium-low heat and use a rubber spatula to gently stir the custard mixture; cook the mixture for 10 to 20 minutes, until it thickens and the little bubbles on the surface have completely disappeared.

Once cooked, pour the custard through a fine mesh sieve into a heat-safe bowl. Add in the lemon zest and stir to combine. Allow the custard to come to room temperature, whisking every 10 to 15 minutes for an hour. Pour the lemon juice into the custard and whisk to combine. Place a piece of plastic wrap onto the surface of the custard and then place it in the refrigerator to chill overnight.

Set up your ice cream maker per the instructions. Once running, slowly stream in the lemon custard. Churn until it looks like soft serve ice cream. Once churned, pour the mixture into the storage container of your choice. I like to line a loaf pan with parchment paper and then place it in the freezer to set for at least 6 hours.

CHRISTMAS | Weihnachten

Christmas is a time for baking and sharing. Whether we share trays of cookies or bottles of *Eierlikör* (page 168) or pass down the recipes to make all of the above, Christmas sweets bring us together. So many recipes that we associate with Germany are part of celebrating Christmas, so it seemed only right to have a chapter dedicated to the holiday season.

For me, Christmas has always been a magical time of year, and at least 50 percent of that time has always been spent in the kitchen with my mom and sister making anything and everything, from iced sugar cookies to our family *Stollen* (page 153). I have been saving my family's Christmas Stollen recipe for this book—it's classic and it felt right to share it with you in this last chapter. I hope at least one of these recipes becomes a new part of your holiday traditions.

CHRISTMAS FRUIT BREAD |
Stollen (*a recipe from my Oma*)

Makes: 2 large stollen loaves

A German Christmas classic! In Germany, Stollen is made only at the holidays, and whether it is purchased at a bakery or your family has been making the same one for generations, everyone has it. If you want to try something traditionally German this year, make this Stollen, but don't forget about it! For the BEST flavor, you have to let these loaves sit in a dark cool room for 3 to 4 weeks so that all the flavors can blend and settle—no peeking and definitely no early tasting!

This recipe has been passed down from my Oma to my mom, and now to me and my sister. We all switch up the dried and candied fruit a little for personal taste but the overall recipe stays the same. It's made from a yeasted dough and filled to the brim with rum-soaked fruits and toasted chopped nuts, but my favorite part is the icing layer. It's made when the butter melts onto the hot loaves soon after baking and is then topped with a thick layer of powdered sugar that mixes with the butter to make a sweet and delicious topping.

Active Time: 1 hour 30 minutes

Total Time: 3–4 weeks

---

80 g (½ cup + 1 tbsp) raisins

80 g (⅔ cup) dried cranberries

80 g (½ cup) dried tart cherries, roughly chopped

80 g (½ cup + 2 tbsp) dried apricots, roughly chopped

100 g (3.5 oz) candied lemon peel, chopped

100 g (3.5 oz) candied orange peel, chopped

120 ml (½ cup) rum

120 g (1 cup + 1½ tbsp) pecans, toasted and chopped

700 g (5½ cups + 1½ tbsp) all-purpose flour

200 g (1 cup) granulated sugar

20 g (1 tbsp + 2 tsp) instant yeast (2½ packets)

250 ml (1 cup + 2 tsp) milk, lukewarm

2 large eggs, room temperature

60 g (¼ cup) butter, softened

1 tsp vanilla extract

1 lemon, zested

In a medium-sized bowl, add in the raisins, dried cranberries, dried tart cherries, dried apricots, candied lemon and orange peel, and then top the dried fruit mixture with the rum. Stir to combine everything, cover the bowl, and leave it to sit overnight. The next day, stir in the toasted and chopped pecans.

Once the fruit has soaked overnight, whisk together the flour, sugar, and yeast, in the bowl of a stand mixer. Add in the lukewarm milk, eggs, butter, vanilla and lemon zest. Use the dough hook to knead the dough together until it is fully kneaded. The dough should be smooth and the edges of the bowl should be clean. Place the dough into a large greased bowl, which can be the same mixing bowl, and then cover with a lid or plastic wrap.

Leave the dough to proof somewhere warm for 45 minutes to an hour until it has doubled in size. Pour in the fruits and knead until they are fully combined. Cover again and leave to sit for 15 minutes. Line two baking sheets with parchment paper or silicone baking mats.

Sprinkle the dough and your work surface with flour. Scoop the dough onto the work surface. Divide the dough into two equal portions.

Pat each portion into a rectangle that is approximately 14 x 12 inches (36 x 31 cm). With the rectangle in front of you 14 inches (36 cm) long and 12 inches (30.5 cm) wide, fold slightly more than the left third of the dough over the middle portion of the dough, stopping it 3 inches (8 cm) from the edge of the opposite side of the rectangle.

Press an indentation, lengthwise, 3 inches (8 cm) in from the folded edge of the dough. Place one loaf onto each lined baking sheet and drape them with a sheet of plastic wrap or kitchen towels. Leave the dough to proof for 1 hour. While the dough proofs, preheat the oven to 325°F (163°C) and arrange two racks in the oven so that it splits the oven into thirds.

(continued)

120 ml (½ cup) butter, melted

300 g (2½ cups) powdered sugar
more as needed

Once proofed, remove the drape on top, and bake both stollens in the preheated oven for 30 minutes. After 30 minutes have passed, swap the pans and rotate them 180 degrees. Bake for another 15 minutes, until they are a deep golden brown. If they are looking pale, bake for another 5–10 minutes.

Once baked, take the pans out of the oven and place them on wire racks. Leave the loaves to cool for 5 minutes before brushing the tops with the melted butter. Use up all of the butter. Sift the powdered sugar over the top of the stollen loaves until it stops sinking in. Leave to sit for 1 hour. If there are any patches where the powdered sugar has absorbed into the butter, dust them with more powdered sugar.

Leave the loaves to cool completely. Once cooled, wrap the loaves in aluminum foil and then place them in large plastic bags. Seal the bags or tie the ends in knots. Place them somewhere dark and cool and leave to sit for 3 to 4 weeks. Unwrap and slice them with a serrated knife.

Notes

As mentioned in the description, you can switch up what dried fruit you put in the loaves—just make sure the total weight is still the same!

The alcohol will bake out but for an alcohol-free version, soak the dried fruit mixture in water with a little vanilla extract.

LEBKUCHEN, JAM & MARZIPAN BITES | Dominos

Servings: 32

If you've never had a Domino or *dominostein*, you're missing out. It doesn't matter if you don't like marzipan—the way the three layers of these bite-sized sweets go together, especially with the dark chocolate coating, is simply magical.

If I'm being honest, I usually buy them at the store, but they aren't always available. So for the times you can't buy them, make them. Dominos are made with a thin layer of *lebkuchen*, topped with a layer of set jam, usually red currant or apricot, finished off with a layer of marzipan and then coated in a thin layer of dark chocolate. They're basically everything you could want, all in one bite.

Active Time: 1 hour
Total Time: 24 hours

Lebkuchen Layer
35 g (2½ tbsp) butter
20 ml (1 tbsp + 1 tsp) honey
35 g (2½ tbsp) brown sugar
20 ml (1 tbsp + 1 tsp) milk
1 tsp ground cinnamon
¾ tsp ground ginger
¼ tsp ground cloves
¼ tsp allspice
¼ tsp ground nutmeg
40 g (⅓ cup) all-purpose flour
½ tsp baking powder

Jam Layer
50 ml (2 tbsp + 2 tsp) water
7–8 g powdered gelatin (1 packet)
325 g (1 cup + 1 tsp) apricot or red currant jam

Lebkuchen Layer

Preheat the oven to 350°F (177°C) and place a rack in the center of the oven. Lightly grease a 9 x 5–inch (23 x 13–cm) loaf pan with baking spray or softened butter. Lay a piece of 9 x 15–inch (23 x 38–cm) parchment paper down one long side, across the bottom and back up the other side. The grease will help the paper stick.

In a medium-sized sauce pot, add in the butter, honey, brown sugar, milk, cinnamon, ginger, ground cloves, allspice and nutmeg. Melt the mixture over medium heat, stirring frequently with a rubber spatula. If it looks separated and strange once heated, the milk has split and it needs to be done again—this can happen if it is not stirred enough at the beginning. Once melted and just starting to bubble, take the pot off the heat. Pour the mixture into a medium-sized mixing bowl and mix on medium, with a handheld mixer or a stand mixer with the whisk attachment, for about one minute.

Add in the flour and baking powder and mix again until the ingredients are just combined. Pour the batter into the lined pan and spread them out to create an even layer. Bake the lebkuchen in the preheated oven for 13 to 15 minutes, until it appears a little dry and set on top.

Once baked, take the pan out of the oven and place it on a wire rack to cool completely. Once cooled, gently lift the cake base out with the parchment paper, just to loosen it. Reline the pan with a sheet of plastic wrap that goes up all four sides and put just the cake back in the pan.

Jam Layer

In a medium-sized, heat-safe bowl, add in the water and sprinkle the powdered gelatin over the top. Stir together and set this aside.

Strain the jam you are using into a small sauce pot. To make sure there are no bits or clumps, it may need to be slightly warmed up to do so. Heat the jam over medium heat, stirring frequently until it is just bubbling. Remove it from the heat and pour it into the bowl with the bloomed gelatin. Stir to combine.

(continued)

Marzipan Layer

225 g (1 cup) marzipan

Chocolate Coating

300 g (10.6 oz) 60% dark
chocolate, chopped

Note

These are best stored in the refrigerator, for at least a week, to keep the
layers together and to prevent the
chocolate from melting.

Continue to stir the mixture every 15 minutes, until it just begins to
thicken. This can take up to a couple of hours, but the process can be
sped up by putting it in the refrigerator and then stirring it far more
often to prevent the gelatin from setting unevenly and clumping along
the edges.

Once it starts to thicken, set it aside and immediately move on to the
Marzipan Layer.

Marzipan Layer

Knead the marzipan slightly, by hand, so it is easier to work with. Then
roll it out, using a little powdered sugar to keep it from sticking to the
size of the bottom of the pan. Pour the thickened jam mixture over the
lebkuchen layer. Quickly and carefully lift up the marzipan layer and
place it on top of the jam. Place the whole pan in the refrigerator and
leave it to set overnight.

Once set, use the plastic wrap to lift the assembled cake out of the
pan and then peel it away. Use a sharp thin knife to trim off any messy
edges, cleaning the knife between each cut.

Cut the cake in half horizontally. Then, cut each shorter piece into four
rows lengthwise and four rows horizontally.

Place the individual squares on a parchment-lined tray or plate that will
fit in your freezer and freeze for about an hour to help them hold together.

Melt the dark chocolate in a medium-sized microwave-safe bowl or in
a sauce pot. Get out two trays, place a silicone mat or parchment paper
on one and find something small that one domino can sit on at a time to
hold it away from the second tray, like a little pedestal.

Once frozen, only take a few of the dominos out of the freezer at a time.
Place one at a time onto something that is smaller than the base of the
domino. I used a mini round cookie cutter but anything will work as
long as it can balance the domino and is smaller than the base.

Chocolate Coating

Pour the melted chocolate over the top and use a dinner knife or the
back of a spoon to smooth the chocolate across all four sides. The excess
chocolate will run onto the tray and can later be reheated and reused
if you run out of chocolate. Lift the now coated domino with a spatula
or two dinner knives on their sides and place it onto the lined baking
sheet to set. Continue this process until all dominos are coated. Place
back in the fridge to store.

ANGEL EYES | Engelsaugen

The quintessential Christmas cookie, similar to a thumbprint cookie, these soft butter cookies are shaped into balls, dimpled in the center, and baked with the jam already in them rather than with the jam added into the dimples after baking. The cookies are extra light and soft because they are made with powdered sugar instead of granulated sugar in the dough. The jam being baked with the cookie means that some of the moisture bakes out and it becomes an even more intense burst of flavor. They're so simple and easy that they don't need much of an introduction, but they are always a crowd-pleaser because who doesn't love a butter cookie with a little dollop of your favorite jam?

Active Time: 30 minutes
Total Time: 2 hours

---

150 g (⅔ cup) butter, softened

100 g (¾ cup + 1 tbsp) powdered sugar

2 egg yolks

1 tsp vanilla extract

¼ tsp almond extract

250 g (2 cups) all-purpose flour

100 g (¼ cup + 1 tbsp) raspberry jam

50 g (⅓ cup + 1 tbsp) powdered sugar, for dusting, optional

In the bowl of a stand mixer, add in the butter, powdered sugar, egg yolks and both extracts. Use the paddle attachment to cream them together on low speed and then on medium speed until the mixture is smooth and creamy.

Scrape the sides of the bowl with a rubber spatula and add in the all-purpose flour. Mix again until the flour is just combined. Press the dough together into a ball, place in a sheet of plastic wrap and chill in the refrigerator for an hour. Preheat the oven to 350°F (177°C) and place two racks in the oven so that they divide it into thirds. Line two baking sheets with parchment paper or silicone baking mats.

Divide the dough into 25-gram (1-oz) portions and roll them into smooth balls. Space them evenly across both baking sheets. Use a round teaspoon scoop to press into the top of each ball of dough and create an indentation. Place the cookies back in the refrigerator for 30 minutes.

Once chilled, take the cookies out of the refrigerator. Spoon slightly less than 1 teaspoon of jam into the indentation of each cookie.

Bake in the preheated oven for 7 minutes. After 7 minutes, swap the baking sheets and rotate them 180 degrees. Bake for another 7 minutes. Once baked and just barely golden brown on the bottom edge, take the baking sheets out of the oven and place them on wire racks to cool. Optionally, dust the cookies with powdered sugar once they are cooled.

Note

It's ok to fill the dimple completely with jam—just don't overfill them or the jam will bubble up and run down the side. On the other hand, because the jam reduces slightly while baking, you don't want to underfill it because you'll be left with very little. (I've found that just under 1 teaspoon of jam is the perfect amount.)

CANDIED ALMONDS | Gebrannte Mandeln

Servings: 12

One of my favorite memories of summers spent in Germany was going up to the carts in the squares that sold *Gebrannte Mandeln*, buying a little bag and eating them with my mom and sister until our stomachs hurt. You could smell the warm cinnamon and roasting nuts the moment you came within 50 feet of the carts, and once we smelled them, we couldn't *not* have them. Candied almonds, also known as Gebrannte Mandeln in Germany, are simple but delicious with a candied cinnamon sugar coating around crunchy roasted almonds—what could be better? When I lived in NYC, one of my favorite parts about the winter months were the carts that sold candied almonds because I would smell them walking down the sidewalk and instantly be transported back to some of my happiest memories.

Active Time: 25 minutes

Total Time: 25 minutes

---

100 g (½ cup) granulated sugar, divided

100 g (⅓ cup + 2 tbsp) brown sugar

2 tsp (6 g) cinnamon

100 ml (⅓ cup + 1 tbsp + 1 tsp) water

200 g (1⅓ cups + 1 tbsp) almonds

Line a baking sheet with a piece of parchment paper and set aside. In a large shallow pan, add in approximately half of the white sugar, all of the brown sugar and the cinnamon. Stir this together with a wooden spoon. Add in the water and stir again. Place the mixture over medium-high heat and bring to a gentle boil.

Once it starts to bubble all over, add in the almonds and stir to coat them. Reduce the heat slightly—it should still be bubbling. Continue stirring and cooking until all of the liquid has cooked out. It will look as though the sugar is dry and crumbly. Slightly reduce the heat again. Depending on your stove, it should now be around medium or just below.

The sugar will start to caramelize and liquify as it heats and you continue to stir. Don't stop stirring or the sugar will burn. Once about half of the sugar has turned into caramel, sprinkle the remaining sugar over the almonds and stir together. Cook for about 30 seconds until the new sugar is mixed in but not caramelized. Immediately pour the candied almonds onto the parchment-lined baking sheet. Separate the almonds with two utensils and leave to cool fully.

Notes

Be sure to have all of the ingredients measured out and everything ready to go before starting this recipe. Once the cooking starts, you don't want to walk away.

These are delicious when warm, but be sure to let them cool fully before storing in an airtight container. These can be stored at room temperature in an airtight container for at least a few weeks.

CANDIED ALMOND ELISEN LEBKUCHEN | Gebrannte Mandel Elisen Lebkuchen

Makes: 18 cookies

If you want to know my favorite German Christmas cookie, this is it. I absolutely LOVE these *Gebrannte Mandeln Elisen Lebkuchen*. They're spiced but still sweet, soft and chewy, not too dense, and topped with a layer of dark chocolate and candied almonds. I mean, how could they get much better?

There are endless types of *lebkuchen*, from crunchy and crispy cookies with icing to soft and pillowy lebkuchen, each one coming from a different region or family in Germany. *Elisen Lebkuchen* are made with ground nuts instead of flour; they're chewy, sweet and full of spiced holiday flavor. I recently had this variation with Gebrannte Mandeln (roasted, candied almonds, page 160) and knew I had to share the recipe with you!

Active Time: 45 minutes

Total Time: 1 hour 30 minutes

Cookies

18 (2¾-inch [7-cm]) back oblaten

3 large eggs

14 ml (1 tbsp) honey

80 g (⅓ cup + ½ tbsp) brown sugar

125 g (1 cup) hazelnuts, finely ground

100 g (1 cup + 1 tbsp) almond flour

35 g (1.2 oz) Gebrannte Mandeln (page 160), roughly chopped

6 g (2 tsp) ground cinnamon

2 g (1½ tsp) ground ginger

1 tsp allspice

1 tsp ground cloves

½ tsp ground nutmeg

80 g (2.8 oz) candied lemon peel, finely chopped

80 g (2.8 oz) candied orange peel, finely chopped

Topping

250 g (8.8 oz) 60% dark chocolate, roughly chopped

75 g (2.6 oz) Gebrannte Mandeln (page 160), finely chopped

Cookies

Preheat the oven to 350°F (177°C) and place two racks in the oven so that they divide it into thirds. Line two baking sheets with parchment paper or silicone baking mats. Evenly space nine of the back oblaten wafers onto each baking sheet.

In the bowl of a stand mixer, add in the eggs, honey and brown sugar. Use the whisk attachment to whip on high until they are frothy for 2 to 3 minutes. In a separate bowl, stir together the ground hazelnuts, almond flour, roughly chopped Gebrannte Mandeln (page 160), cinnamon, ginger, allspice, ground cloves and nutmeg. Pour the nut mixture into the egg mixture. Use a rubber spatula to combine the ingredients until everything is fully mixed. Then, pour in the finely chopped candied lemon and orange peels and stir them to combine.

Pour the cookie mixture into a piping bag and pipe them onto each wafer cookie, starting in the center and working outward in a spiral to the outer edge. The cookie mixture should be between ¾-inch (2-cm) and 1-inch (2.5-cm) thick and cover the wafer all the way to the edge. Bake the cookies in the preheated oven for 9 minutes. After 9 minutes swap the baking sheets and rotate them 180 degrees. Bake the cookies for another 9 minutes. Once baked, remove the baking sheets from the oven and place them on wire racks to cool fully.

Topping

Pour the roughly chopped chocolate into a medium-sized microwave-safe bowl and melt in the microwave, stirring after every 15 seconds. Once melted, pour the chopped Gebrannte Mandeln into the chocolate and stir to combine.

Working one cooled cookie at a time, hold on to the edges and flip the cookie over. Dip the top of the cookie into the melted chocolate mixture to the bottom edges—it's ok that your fingertips get in the chocolate. Lift the cookie out and shake it back and forth to get rid of the extra chocolate. Flip the cookie back over and place it back on the lined baking sheet until the chocolate has set.

Note

If you can't find back oblaten wafers that are 2¾ inches (7 cm) at your store, they can be ordered online!

SLICE & BAKE VANILLA BUTTER COOKIES | Heidesand

You know those simple butter cookies that might seem kind of boring until you take a bite and then they melt in your mouth and have the most delicious, sweet, buttery flavor? That's these German *Heidesand* cookies.

Most cultures seem to have a simple vanilla butter cookie at the holidays, and Heidesand are one of my favorites. These are often made with browned butter, but my family likes to keep it simple and make them without. Heidesand are a simple slice and bake cookie that are rolled in sugar for a little crunchy edge and are perfect for dipping in hot coffee or hot chocolate. They're simple and they're easy—perfect for the bustling holiday season!

Active Time: 20 minutes

Total Time: 24 hours

200 g (¾ cup + 2 tbsp) butter, softened

100 g (¾ cup + 1 tbsp) powdered sugar

30 ml (2 tbsp) milk

1 tsp vanilla extract

¼ tsp almond extract

250 g (2 cups) all-purpose flour

50 g (¼ cup) granulated sugar

In the bowl of a stand mixer, add in the butter, powdered sugar, milk and both extracts. Cream the ingredients together with the paddle attachment on low for 2 to 3 minutes, until the mixture is combined and smooth. Pour in the flour and mix again until just combined.

Lay out two sheets of plastic wrap and equally divide the dough onto both sheets. Use the plastic wrap to roll each portion into a log that is approximately 1½ inches (4 cm) in diameter. Once wrapped tightly, wrap each roll in aluminum foil for stability and put in the refrigerator to chill overnight.

Preheat the oven to 350°F (177°C) and place two racks in the oven so it is divided into thirds. Line two baking sheets with parchment paper or silicone baking mats. Sprinkle a cutting board with the granulated sugar. Unroll one log of cookie and firmly press it into the sugar, roll the log in the sugar so that it is evenly coated all over. Use a sharp knife to slice the roll into ¼-inch (6-mm) thick slices and place them on the lined baking sheets with about ¾ inch (2 cm) of space between them. Repeat with the second log of dough.

Bake the cookies in the preheated oven for 6 minutes. After 6 minutes, swap the baking sheets and rotate them 180 degrees. Bake for another 6 minutes. They won't change much in color. Once baked, remove the sheets from the oven and place them on wire racks to cool fully.

Notes

Do not skip the chilling time or the cookie dough won't hold together properly.

Once baked, these can be stored at room temperature in an airtight container for a few weeks.

ALMOND MARZIPAN COOKIES | Mandelhörnchen

This one is for the almond and marzipan lovers, and in Germany there are a lot of them, so obviously there had to be a marzipan cookie in this cookbook. I didn't think I would like these—I'm not a huge marzipan lover but after making these, I couldn't stop eating them, ESPECIALLY the little ends dipped in dark chocolate because almonds and dark chocolate go together like bread and butter. All that is to say, if you're even considering trying them, do it!

Don't be fooled by the appearance, these *Mandelhörnchen* are soft and chewy and full of marzipan flavor. They are often found at bakeries and made to be four times the size, but I find this size to be much more manageable at home and better for sharing at the holidays!

Active Time: 30 minutes

Total Time: 1 hour

Dough

2 egg whites

400 g (1¾ cups) marzipan

250 g (2 cups + 1 tbsp) powdered sugar

300 g (2¼ cups + 1 tbsp) almond flour

30 ml (2 tbsp) lemon juice

Toppings

1 egg white

200 g (1¾ cups + 1 tbsp) sliced almonds, roughly chopped

140 g (4.9 oz) 60% dark chocolate, roughly chopped

Dough

Preheat the oven to 350°F (177°C) and place two racks in the oven so that they divide it into thirds. Line two baking sheets with parchment paper or silicone baking mats. In the bowl of a stand mixer, add in the 2 egg whites and marzipan torn into little bits. Use the paddle attachment to mix together on medium speed until it is smooth and creamy. Add in the powdered sugar, almond flour and lemon juice and mix again until fully combined.

Portion the dough into 45-gram (1.6-oz) balls. The dough will be sticky, so wet your hands as needed. Shape each ball into a log that is about 3 inches (8-cm) long and place on the lined baking sheets.

Topping

Put the remaining egg white into a small bowl, big enough for each log to dip into. Pour the chopped, sliced almonds into a separate bowl. Working with one log at a time, dip it into the egg white and then into the sliced almonds to coat the cookie fully. Gently curve the log into a crescent or U-shape and place ten on each baking sheet.

Bake the cookies in the preheated oven for 8 minutes, then swap the baking sheets, rotate them 180 degrees and bake them for another 4 to 7 minutes, until they are just lightly colored and starting to look dry on the surface. Once baked, take the pans out of the oven and place them on wire racks to cool completely.

Once fully cooled, melt the chocolate in a microwave-safe bowl or in a sauce pot on the stove. Dip both ends of each cookie, about ¾ inch (2 cm) down, into the chocolate. Shake them gently back and forth to allow the excess chocolate to drip off and then place them back on the lined baking sheets to set. If you are in a hurry or your space is warm, put the chocolate-dipped cookies in the refrigerator to help the chocolate set faster.

Notes

This dough is sticky but it shouldn't be too sticky to shape; if it is, add a little more almond flour to the dough before shaping them.

They are traditionally dipped in dark chocolate, and I think they taste best with the dark chocolate to balance out the sweet richness, but you can of course omit the chocolate if you prefer.

EGG & RUM LIQUEUR | Eierlikör

Makes: 1 pint (473 ml)

German egg liqueur—if you've never had it, you're probably thinking, "Audrey, why would I drink raw egg yolks?" But hear me out, *Eierlikör* is usually enjoyed at the holidays and is made with just five ingredients, including rum (which helps preserve the egg yolks and prevent bacteria) and egg yolks (which make it creamy and delicious). It's very strong, unlike eggnog, but it can be sipped on or used in desserts like the Eierlikör Walnut Cake (page 175). If you are in Germany, it's easy to go to the store and get a bottle, but it can be difficult to find in the US, so here's a simple recipe!

Active Time: 30 minutes

Total Time: 30 minutes

4 egg yolks

1 tsp vanilla extract

100 g (¾ cup + 1 tbsp) powdered sugar

240 ml (1 cup) heavy cream

120 ml (½ cup) rum (brown or clear)

In the bowl of a stand mixer, add in the egg yolks, vanilla and powdered sugar. Use the whisk attachment to whisk on high for 10 minutes (start on low). This may seem like overkill but you will notice the difference later on.

Turn the mixer down to medium-low and stream in the heavy cream down the side of the bowl. Whisk again on high until lines appear. Turn down the mixer again and stream in the rum. Return the mixer to high and mix again for another 3 minutes. Pour the Eierlikör in a sanitized jar with a lid and store in your refrigerator for 1 to 2 weeks. If it separates, just shake it until combined.

Note

This is made with raw egg yolks, so I recommend using fresh eggs.

SPICED CUTOUT COOKIES |
Gewürz Spekulatius

Makes: 24 (3–inch [8–cm]) cookies

Perfectly thin, melt-in-your-mouth spiced cookies. Growing up we ALWAYS had *Gewürz Spekulatius* in our pantry. Basically, there's regular Spekulatius which have a little bit of spice and flavor, and then there's Gewürz Spekulatius which have an extra kick of spices and flavor in them. Every year, we would ration them until the next holiday season to make sure we didn't run out before we could get them again, because they're just so good.

You can eat them plain, dip them in a cup of hot tea, and least traditionally, but one of my favorites, use them instead of graham crackers for the most delicious s'mores in the summer. Plus, there's something so fun and satisfying about re-creating one of your favorite store-bought treats because it guarantees that you will never run out again.

Active Time: 30 minutes

Total Time: 1 hour 45 minutes

---

150 g (⅔ cup) butter, softened

150 g (⅔ cup + 1 tsp) brown sugar

1 egg yolk

1 tsp vanilla extract

¼ tsp almond extract

1½ tsp (6 g) ground cinnamon

½ tsp ground cardamom

¼ tsp ground cloves

¼ tsp ground anise seed

250 g (2 cups) all-purpose flour

1 tsp baking powder

In the bowl of a stand mixer, add in the butter, brown sugar, egg yolk, both extracts, cinnamon, cardamom, ground cloves and anise.

Use the paddle attachment to cream them together on low speed and then on medium speed until they are smooth and creamy.

Scrape the sides of the bowl with a rubber spatula, then add in the all-purpose flour and baking powder. Mix again until the dough is just combined. Dump the dough out onto a sheet of plastic wrap and wrap it up tight into a disk that is 1 inch (2.5 cm) thick. Place it in the refrigerator for at least 1 hour to chill.

Preheat the oven to 350°F (177°C) and place two racks in the oven so that they divide it into thirds. Line two baking sheets with parchment paper or silicone baking mats.

Once chilled, roll the dough out on a lightly floured surface until it is ⅛ inch (3 mm) thick. Use a cookie cutter of your choice to cut out the cookies. With a spatula, gently lift the cutout cookies and place them on the lined baking sheets. Gently bring the extra dough back together into a cohesive disk. Chill while the first batch bakes and then roll the dough out again and cut out a second round of cookies.

Bake in the preheated oven for 6 minutes. After 6 minutes, swap the baking sheets and rotate 180 degrees. Bake for another 4 to 6 minutes, until the edges have darkened slightly. Once baked, take the baking sheets out of the oven and place them on wire racks to cool until the cookies are room temperature and can be moved.

Notes

Because these cookies are thin, they bake quickly. Keep an eye out for the edges. They should darken slightly but not more than that.

If you love chocolate, these are delicious dipped halfway in melted dark chocolate.

CHOCOLATE SPRITZ COOKIES
Schokolade Spritzgebäck

Makes: 72 (1-inch [2.5-cm]) cookies

Classic spritz cookies are great, but so is this chocolate version, because what is a day without chocolate? They're chocolatey the way that chocolate shortbread is—it's not overly rich or sweet, but the cocoa powder adds just the right amount of chocolate to these otherwise simple, holiday cookies.

One of the most fun parts about spritz cookies is that you can make them any shape you want. I'm a classic girl at heart, so I tend to stick with little kisses, but you can pipe or spritz anything from Christmas trees to wreaths and everything in between. If for some reason, delicious flaked salt with chocolate isn't your thing, adding sprinkles or a drizzle of white chocolate to the dark chocolate dip are also delicious options.

Active Time: 30 minutes

Total Time: 1 hour

Dough

125 g (½ cup + 1 tbsp) butter, softened

125 g (½ cup + 1 tbsp + 2 tsp) granulated sugar

1 large egg, room temperature

1 tsp vanilla extract

88 ml (⅓ cup + ½ tbsp) heavy cream

40 g (¼ cup + 3 tbsp) cocoa powder, natural or Dutch processed

225 g (1¾ cups + 1 tbsp) all-purpose flour

¼ tsp baking powder

Chocolate Coating

200 g (7 oz) 60% dark chocolate

Flaky sea salt, optional

Notes

If the dough is too hard to pipe, it may be too cold. Hold the bag in your hands and massage the dough a little to warm it up before trying to pipe the cookies.

If flaky sea salt isn't your thing, sprinkle on chocolate sprinkles, regular sprinkles or leave them blank!

Dough

Preheat the oven to 350°F (177°C) and place two racks in the oven so that they divide it into thirds. Line two baking sheets with parchment paper or silicone baking mats. In the bowl of a stand mixer, add in the butter, sugar, egg, vanilla extract, heavy cream and cocoa powder. Use paddle attachment to cream the ingredients together, starting low and ending on medium speed until they are just combined. Scrape down the sides and bottom of the bowl with a rubber spatula. Then, add in the flour and baking powder and mix again until the ingredients are just combined.

Fit a piping bag with a star tip or use a spritz tool. Put about a quarter of the chocolate dough into the piping bag and squeeze it down to the bottom. Twist the bag just above the dough to create pressure on the dough.

Holding the piping bag vertically, pipe the cookie dough onto the lined baking sheets, pressing down slightly so the cookie goes out instead of up. Pipe them into your desired shape. Leave about ½ inch (1 cm) of space between each cookie. Then, repeat with the remaining dough.

Bake the cookies in the preheated oven. After 7 minutes, swap the baking sheets and rotate them 180 degrees. Bake for another 5 minutes, until the surface is dry. Once baked, remove the baking sheets and place them on wire racks to cool. Allow the cookies to cool fully before dipping them in chocolate.

Chocolate Coating

Melt the chocolate in a microwave-safe bowl, in 10–15 second increments, or in a sauce pot on the stove. Dip one cookie at a time halfway into the melted chocolate. Shake the cookie back and forth to allow the excess chocolate to drip off. Place the cookie back on the lined baking sheet and optionally sprinkle with flaky sea salt. Repeat with the remaining cookies. Leave them to sit until the chocolate has set.

EIERLIKÖR WALNUT CAKE | Eierlikör Walnusskuchen

Servings: 8–12

Eierlikör (page 168) is a German liqueur often had around the holidays that is made from egg yolks, powdered sugar, heavy cream and rum. This cake came to me after I was recently in a museum in Germany and in the café, there was a hazelnut Eierlikör cake. I loved the idea of mixing such a strong liqueur with toasted nuts to create a wintertime cake.

Since Eierlikör is traditionally consumed around Christmas time, I wanted the other flavors in the cake to mimic that. There is warm cinnamon in the walnut cake, along with a layer of plum butter that is made from the end of summer plums and Eierlikör and nutmeg in the whipped cream. This cake packs a punch of flavor for how simple it is!

Active Time: 45 minutes
Total Time: 6 hours

200 g (1½ cups + 1½ tbsp) all-purpose flour

250 g (1¼ cups) granulated sugar

1 tsp baking soda

1 tsp baking powder

2 tsp (6 g) ground cinnamon

6 eggs, room temperature

200 g (¾ cup + 2 tbsp) unsalted butter, softened

1 tsp vanilla extract

150 g (1¾ cups + 2 tbsp) walnuts, finely ground

100 g (¾ cup + 1 tbsp) walnuts, roughly chopped

Preheat the oven to 350°F (177°C) and place a rack in the center of the oven. In the bowl of a stand mixer, whisk together the flour, sugar, baking soda, baking powder and cinnamon. Add in the eggs, butter and vanilla. Use the paddle attachment to mix the batter starting on low and quickly increasing the speed to high. Mix for 2 minutes, until the batter is light and fluffy.

Remove the bowl from the mixer and pour in all of the walnuts. Use a rubber spatula to fold in the nuts.

Line a 9-inch (23-cm) springform pan (a 9-inch [23-cm] metal cake pan will work too) with a baking spray that includes flour—just be sure to not overspray it or let much come up the sides of the pan. Alternatively, you can lightly grease the base with butter and then lay a circle of parchment paper on top.

Pour the cake batter into the pan and place the cake in the preheated oven. Set the timer for 20 minutes. After 20 minutes have passed, rotate the pan 180 degrees and bake for another 15 minutes, until it is golden brown and a toothpick inserted in the center of the cake comes out clean. Once baked, remove the cake from the oven and place on a wire rack to cool for at least 10 to 15 minutes.

Run a knife along the edge between the cake and the pan to make sure that it didn't stick anywhere and then release the springform. Leave the cake to cool fully to room temperature and store in the refrigerator until it is cold and you are ready to assemble the cake.

(continued)

300 ml (1¼ cups) heavy cream, cold

½ tsp nutmeg

100 g (¾ cup + 1 tbsp) powdered sugar

60 ml (4 tbsp) Eierlikör (page 168), plus more for drizzling

100 g (⅓ cup + 1 tbsp + 1 tsp) plum butter

In the bowl of a stand mixer, pour in the cold heavy cream, nutmeg and powdered sugar. Use the whisk attachment to whisk the mixture on low until the powdered sugar is mixed in and then turn the speed to medium-high. Whisk until soft peaks form and then pour in the Eierlikör. Whisk on high until stiff peaks form. Place the bowl in the refrigerator and move on to assembling the cake.

Using a long serrated knife, cut the cooled cake in half into two layers. Spread the plum butter onto the bottom layer. If it is cold and stiff, briefly heat it up in the microwave. Lay the top layer of cake on top of the jam.

Take the whipped cream out of the refrigerator and use a large spoon to dollop the whipped cream onto the center of the cake. Use the back of the spoon to spread the whipped cream within a ½ inch (1.3 cm) of the edge of the cake. Optionally, drizzle more Eierlikör over the top of the whipped cream. The whipped cream will be soft if served immediately but it will stiffen slightly if it sits in the refrigerator for a few hours.

Notes

To make an alcohol-free version, simply eliminate the Eierlikör from the whipped cream and the drizzle.

If you can't get your hands on plum butter, also known as *powidl, pflaumenmus* or plum jam, you can substitute it with a tart cherry jam.

ALMOND LAYER CAKE | Baumkuchen

Servings: 12–16

Named after the rings on a tree, this cake is made with layers upon layers of thin almond cake baked on top of each other and then coated in a thin layer of melted dark chocolate. It is traditionally made in a special pan that allows the layers to be vertical rather than horizontal, and concentric, starting in the center of the ring and growing outwards as layers are added.

However, most of us don't have access to said pans, so simply follow this method where the layers are horizontal and baked on top of one another in a round or square springform pan. It may seem intimidating, but once you get into the rhythm, it's quite simple and so worth it! I promise there is nothing better than cutting into this cake and seeing every single, individual layer all stacked together.

Active Time: 1 hour 30 minutes

Total Time: 6 hours

---

250 g (1 cup + 2 tbsp) butter, softened, plus extra for lining the pan

150 g (⅔ cup) marzipan

45 ml (3 tbsp) rum (can substitute water)

6 large eggs, cold

200 g (1 cup) granulated sugar

½ tsp almond extract

¼ tsp salt

145 g (1 cup + 2½ tbsp) all-purpose flour

Brush softened butter into the bottom of a 9-inch (23-cm) springform pan and place a 9-inch (23-cm) round of parchment paper into the bottom of the pan. Tear the marzipan into small pieces and add it into a small saucepan with the rum. Heat over medium-low heat and stir until the mixture becomes a thick paste. There should no longer be any chunks of marzipan visible. Pour the mixture into a shallow dish and leave it to cool slightly while preparing the rest of the ingredients.

Separate the 6 eggs. Add the egg whites into one small bowl and the egg yolks into another.

In the bowl of a stand mixer, add in the butter, sugar and almond extract. Use the paddle attachment on medium speed for about 1 minute until light and fluffy. Add two egg yolks at a time to the butter mixture and beat until they are fully incorporated. Continue adding the egg yolks until all have been incorporated, scraping the bowl in between as needed.

Pour half of the slightly chilled marzipan into the butter and egg mixture. Beat to combine and then add in the second half. Pour the mixture into a separate large mixing bowl. Fully clean the bowl of the stand mixer.

Preheat the oven to "broil." If possible, set the broil temperature to 450°F (235°C). Place a rack in the middle of the oven.

Add the egg whites and salt to the clean stand mixer bowl. Use the whisk attachment starting on medium speed to whip the egg whites until they start to become frothy. Then, increase the speed to high and beat for 5 minutes, until stiff peaks form.

Add half of the beaten egg whites into the egg yolk/butter mixture and use a flat rubber spatula to fold the egg whites in until no more white is visible, being careful not to knock all of the air out. Add in the remaining egg whites and fold again to combine. Pour in the all-purpose flour and fold again until no flour is visible.

(continued)

50 g (2½ tbsp) apricot jam

240 g (8.5 oz) 60% dark chocolate

Note

Be sure to watch the cake carefully under the broiler. It can burn very quickly, so you don't want to walk away. Once you start baking the cake, you need to stay by the oven.

Use a ¼-cup (60-ml) measuring cup or weigh out approximately 55 grams (¼ cup) of the batter. Use a spoon to spread the batter into the bottom of the pan. It will be a very thin layer but do your best to spread it evenly across the pan. Place the pan into the oven and broil it for 1 to 3 minutes. I recommend turning the oven light on so that you can watch the layer. Always check the layer after 1 minute to see if it has become golden brown.

Once the surface has at least a few spots that are golden brown, remove the pan and place it on a wire rack. Scoop another heaping 55 grams (¼ cup) of batter on top of the layer that you just baked. I find it easiest to scoop it in four parts into the four corners. Use the back of the spoon to carefully spread the batter out. You will notice it start to melt—that's ok! Use an oven mitt to rotate the pan as needed to carefully spread the batter. Place the pan back in the oven and broil again for 90 to 180 seconds. Try to rotate the pan 90 degrees every time you place it back in the oven so that it browns evenly.

The reason for the range of baking time is that every time the oven door is opened it loses heat. Therefore, the baking time can vary for each layer, so NEVER walk away from it. Continue this layering and baking process until all of the batter has been used. Once the last layer has been broiled, remove the pan from the oven and place it on a wire cooling rack.

Add the apricot jam and 5 milliliters (1 tsp) of water into a microwave-safe bowl, heat for 10 to 15 seconds and then strain through a mesh sieve into another bowl. Use a pastry brush or a spoon to brush the jam/water mixture over the surface of the *baumkuchen* while it's still hot. Once the pan and cake have cooled to room temperature, 3 to 4 hours, remove the springform round.

Place the cooled cake on an upside-down bowl that is smaller than the base of the cake. Chop the dark chocolate into ¼-inch (6-mm) pieces and place in a microwave-safe bowl. Heat in 20-second increments, stirring in between until the chocolate is melted and smooth.

Pour the chocolate over top of the cake in a spiral direction starting from the center and working your way out. Use an offset spatula to spread the chocolate into a flat layer and push the excess chocolate over the sides so that all the edges are covered. Let the excess chocolate drip off the cake. Use the back of the offset spatula to wipe off the excess chocolate from the bottom edge of the cake.

Place the cake in the refrigerator for at least 30 minutes to allow the chocolate to harden. Serve chilled or at room temperature but store in the refrigerator to keep the chocolate from melting.

RUM TRUFFLE TORTE | Rum Trüffeltorte

This is the dessert you make when you have guests coming over for dinner and realize you didn't plan a dessert and aren't going to have oven space or much time to assemble one. It is quite possibly one of the simplest, high-impact desserts you could make.

This Rum Truffle Torte is made from just 6 ingredients including finely ground butter cookies, rum, dark chocolate, butter and a dash of salt. It's based on classic German Rum truffles, it's always a crowd pleaser and there's no need to bake it. Just mix everything together, let it chill and firm up in the refrigerator for a couple hours and you'll be good to go!

Active Time: 30 minutes

Total Time: 2 hours 30 minutes

Truffle

160 g (5.6 oz) butter cookies

90 ml (⅓ cup + 2 tsp) rum

200 g (7.1 oz) 60% dark chocolate

125 g (½ cup + 1 tbsp) butter, softened

½ tsp kosher salt

Topping

30 g (¼ cup + 1½ tbsp) cocoa powder, natural or Dutch processed

Truffle

Roughly crush the butter cookies and put them into a high-powered blender. Blend until they are ground down to a powder. Pour the ground cookies into a medium-sized bowl. Add in the rum and stir to combine and then set aside.

Roughly chop the chocolate, put it in a large microwave-safe bowl and melt in 20-second increments, stirring in between until it is melted. Add the soft butter and salt into the chocolate and stir to combine until all of the butter has melted into the chocolate.

Pour the rum-soaked cookies into the chocolate mixture and stir to combine. Pour the truffle mixture into an 8½-inch (22-cm) removable bottom tart pan or one with a similar area. Place the tart in the refrigerator for 2 hours to set.

Topping

Once set, take the tart out of the refrigerator. Place the pan on a glass or small bowl and remove the rim of the tart pan. Use a spatula to remove the tart from the base and place it on a serving plate. Dust the tart with cocoa powder and serve. It's best if the cake can sit out for 15 minutes prior to serving to soften slightly.

Notes

Because this torte isn't baked, the alcohol is not baked out.

If you want an alcohol-free version, I recommend soaking the cookies in cherry juice for a little extra flavor!

THANK YOU

This book would not exist without my editor, Marissa Giambelluca. Without you, I never would have even considered writing a book. Thank you for believing in me and believing in my goals. Thank you for always answering my millions of questions and working with me until we were both happy with the result. I could not have done this without you and Page Street Publishing.

To my Oma and Opa, thank you for giving me the opportunity to travel and see the world. Thank you for exposing me to amazing food and new experiences, for always letting me pick any pastry I wanted and any cake I couldn't stop staring at. I don't know what I would do without your support and encouragement.

To my parents, I love you and appreciate you both more than you will ever know. Mama, thank you for always answering my questions, for always picking up the phone when I need you, for testing my recipes when I doubt myself and for showing me the love and passion that lies within creating food. Thank you dad, for always being willing to taste test and give honest feedback, for believing in me and for always supporting me when I need it.

To Samantha, my sister, thank you for always being by my side when we would go to bakeries and for holding my hand when I was young and scared. Thank you for protecting me and being an amazing role model for me to look up to. Your hard work and dedication to what you love have influenced me more than you know.

Thank you to my friends who are always there to support me and encourage me when I doubt myself. Thank you to the bakers and *konditors* in Germany for always inspiring new ideas. Thank you to all of you, my community—I wouldn't have written this book without you.

ABOUT THE AUTHOR

Audrey Leonard is a food photographer and recipe developer who loves all things sweet. Her American/German heritage has led her to specialize in German sweets, which she shares the recipes for on her blog, Red Currant Bakery. Audrey has been published in both *ZEITmagazin* and *Bake from Scratch*. With a degree in Fashion Design from FIT in NYC, Audrey focusses on both the taste and the presentation of her treats. When she isn't baking, she's painting, drawing and drinking coffee.

INDEX

D